MINDING THE BEDSIDE
NURSING FROM THE HEART OF THE AWAKENED MIND

MINDING THE BEDSIDE
NURSING FROM THE HEART OF THE AWAKENED MIND

JEROME STONE, MA, RN

LANGDON STREET PRESS

Langdon Street Press
212 3rd Avenue North, Suite 290
Minneapolis, MN 55401
612.455.2293
www.langdonstreetpress.com

ISBN-13: 978-1-936782-46-8
LCCN: 2011932719

Distributed by Itasca Books

Cover Design by Alan Pranke
Typeset by Jill Kennedy

Printed in the United States of America

For my mother, Helaine Stone
and the memory of my father, Noel Stone.
For my sisters, Louisa Stone and Melinda Stone.
And, for my wife, Jill Siegel-Stone,
and son, Noah Siegel-Stone.

Five percent of all proceeds from this book and from all speaking engagements and work derived from this book will be donated to organizations that further the practices of teaching these methods to health-care providers and caretakers of those who are sick and dying. This is my homage to what I have learned and to all those who have chosen to work with their minds and hearts for the benefit of humanity.

Foreword

Minding the Bedside is a rare and timely work of art. Jerome Stone leads us on an illuminating and heart-opening exploration into the true nature of mind, presence, compassion and the healing relationship. Calling on his decades of experience in the nursing profession and his equally rich depth of study of mindfulness and non-dual spirituality, he weaves a magnificent fusion of teachings, stories and insights that will inspire any health care practitioner (not just nurses) to rediscover their art as a blessed opportunity to accelerate their own personal awakening. This book confronts head-on the big questions that all in the helping professions face: What does it mean to "show up", to be present for another? How can I possibly be helpful in the face of unfathomable suffering or impossible circumstances? How can I hold my inner reactivity and what this patient triggers in me? What really is compassion? What is compassionate intention? And perhaps the biggest question of all, What really is this "I" that is doing this work in the first place? To address these questions and others Stone offers his own discoveries as well as gems from many of the world's wisdom traditions, great spiritual teachers, and even scientific research into the nature of mind, meditation and consciousness.

An especially timely contribution is his treatment of the subject of "healing environments" which is gaining traction as a concept for hospitals and other treatment settings to aspire to. For this he argues persuasively that the qualities of mindfulness (focus), meditative awareness (attention) and compassion (caring) in health care personnel are essential to the successful evolution of such programs. Finally, as a practical learning device, the book makes excellent use of summaries of key concepts at the end of each chapter, and provides guided exercises throughout that enable the reader to directly experience the teachings and cultivate the capacity to be a more present, clear and peaceful care provider. *Minding the Bedside* is an outstanding contribution that should be required reading for health care practitioners from all disciplines.

--William Collinge, PhD, Director of the Touch, Caring and Cancer Program and author of *Partners in Healing: Simple Ways to Offer Support, Comfort and Care to a Loved One Facing Illness*

Acknowledgments

Before getting started, it's necessary to acknowledge those who have taught me about directing and engaging my mind in a mindful and compassionate way. I would not be who I am—aware of my strengths and weaknesses—were it not for the thousands of patients who I've worked with in my career. Each one of these individuals—whether in a glance, a touch, an unspoken word, or an outright statement—has taught me how to be more mindful and how to care from the wellspring of the heart. Time and time again, when I've been tired or preoccupied, when my mind has been anywhere but on my patient, it has been the human being in front of me who has brought me back to the task at hand, to the ongoing and uninterrupted presence of my own undistracted mind, and to my compassionate heart.

It has been my patients who have reminded me repeatedly that remaining mindful and compassionate doesn't require enormous effort or have to be overly demanding. All I've needed to do is to see who it is in front of me and focus my presence on them and on their stories, leaving my discursive mind at ease and my own ordinarily distracted mind out of it. In this way, mindfulness has become a learning process where each moment is an opportunity to train my mind and be present and alert. This learning process has permeated my work atmosphere with its wisdom and clarity.

At times, when my heart and mind have been most engaged, I have lost track of myself, of the small me concerned with the schedule, the assignment, the bills waiting at home, or the physical discomfort that I may be feeling at the time. What has emerged has been a transcendent, *almost invisible* "me," informed by and engaged in a more genuine nature of my mind. It is these glimpses while attending to the needs of another that have given me the confidence to continue and to deepen the practices that I present in this book. It has been my patients—their raw, vulnerable, and tender experiences of illness—who have offered me the occasions, these brief but precious glimpses, of a deeper nature beyond my self-referential self.

In addition to my patients, there are unique individuals who have refined their meditative awareness, mindfulness, and compassion and have lived their lives exemplary of their practice. For me, the source of inspiration to work with the distractions and preoccupations of my mind and to dredge up the unsavory sights of judgments and attitudes has been through the stories, teaching, and practices of such individuals. These unique human beings, through their devotion to specific paths, have freed themselves from the claustrophobic entanglements of self-cherishing preoccupation.

While there are numerous individuals who have accomplished this way of being—individuals who I will quote from and refer to in this book and whose work emanates from the realms of spiritual traditions, contemplative practices, poetry, art, and science—the source of most of my inspiration comes from spiritual practitioners, and particularly from Tibetan Buddhism. I would particularly like to pay homage to and thank my teacher, Sogyal Rinpoche, author of *The Tibetan Book of Living and Dying*, who is a profound living example of one who conveys these teachings from a compassionate and unaltered state of mind and from a mind of "being" in these practices. Without his care in presenting many of these teachings to the Western mind, what I have to offer would be—at best—hypothetical and based on conjecture. Instead, I have had the fortunate opportunity to learn from him, to some very basic degree, how to bring my mind home, back to its original nature as a compassionate presence.

I would like to thank all those who helped me with the birthing of this book from ideas flitting as distractions in my mind to the reality of the book that you now hold in your hands. While the list of those to thank would be interminably long were I to include everyone, I'd like to offer special thanks to Susan Ollar, Liz Acosta, Michael Smith, Karl Dickensheets, Darci Meyers, Chris Condon, Barb Rogers, Barb Omdahl, Anne Howland, Whit Pinneo, Russell Duncan, and Fariba Fuller.

Finally, I would first like to thank my family members who have encouraged me through the rigors of my self-doubt and uncertainties. Thanks to my sisters, Louisa Stone and Melinda Stone, who have believed in my visions and have endured my successes as well as my failures throughout the course of our friendship and lives together. I would like to offer a special heartfelt thanks to my wife, Jill Siegel-Stone, for all of her encouragement and support during this process, and my son, Noah Siegel-Stone, for his curiosity about why daddy was writing a book. Keep asking *why*, Noah, and never stop questioning and investigating; it will get you far.

Permissions

I am grateful for the following permissions to use previously copyrighted material:

Excerpts from *A Sense of the Cosmos* by Jacob Needleman. Copyright © 1965 Monkfish Publishing, Rhinebeck, NY. Used with permission of the publisher.

Excerpts from *A Vow of Conversation; Journals 1964-1964*, by Thomas Merton. Copyright © 1999 Farrar, Straus & Giroux New York, NY. Used with permission of the publisher.

Excerpts from *Christian Meditation: Experiencing the Presence of God* by James Finley. Copyright © 2004 HarperCollins Publishers, New York, NY. Used with the permission of the publisher.

"The Ethic of Compassion", from *Ethics for the New Millennium* by Dalai Lama and Alexander Norman, copyright © 1999 by His Holiness the Dalai Lama. Used by permission of the Riverhead Books, an imprint of Penguin Group (USA) Inc..

Excerpts from *Facing Death and Finding Hope: A Guide to the Emotional and Spiritual Care of the Dying* by Christine Longaker. Copyright © 1997 Random House Publishers, New York, NY. Used with the permission of the publisher.

Excerpts from *Full Catastrophe Living: Using the Wisdom of your Body and Mind to Face Stress, Pain, and Illness* by Jon Kabat-Zinn. Copyright © 1990 Random House Publishers, New York, NY. Used with the permission of the publisher.

Excerpts from *Glimpse After Glimpse* by Sogyal Rinpoche. Copyright © 1995 HarperCollins Publishers, New York, NY. Used with the permission of the publisher.

Reprinted by permission of the publisher from *Healing Spaces: The Sci-*

Contents

Introduction   xv

Chapter 1: Motivation   1

Chapter 2: Riding the Breath to the Meditative Mind   9

Chapter 3: Who's Minding the Bedside?   21

Chapter 4: Compassion   39

Chapter 5: Working with Our Thoughts   55

Chapter 6: Mindfulness Is Not Enough   67

Chapter 7: Alone with Our Thoughts   77

Chapter 8: How Do I Become So Distracted?   85

Chapter 9: Who Is Doing the Attending?   91

Chapter 10: Another You   99

Chapter 11: If Not Now, When?   111

Chapter 12: Research Into Meditation and the Mind   119

Chapter 13: Mind—the Forerunner of a Healing Environment   129

Chapter 14: Ending with the End   137

Chapter 15: Meeting the Road   147

Appendices   159

Resources   165

Sources   181

Index   199

Think of me as a signpost,
pointing the way.
Not the destination,
but a marker on the path.

Think of me as a mirror,
no inherent brilliance of my own.
Reflecting back your mind's wisdom,
for you to see.

Think of me as a dream,
the projection of mind.
Coming to you with a message,
symbols of your own inherent mind.

- Jerome Stone, 2008

Introduction

Who are you when you show up at the bedside? Are you excited? Burned out? Distracted? Energetic? Poetic? Sleeping? Maybe a combination of all of these? Or does it depend on what day it is? Or, hadn't you even thought about it? When we show up at the bedside and we're with our patients, we need to be there, present, alert, and compassionate! What happens, though, is that overwork, compassion-fatigue, distraction, and burnout take our vital presence away from those who need it the most and leave us feeling less than rewarded in our work. What we need is a way to make sure that we're showing up completely at the bedside.

I suspect that there is not one person in health care that has not, at one time or another, found their mind drifting away from their patient even though their genuine interest was to serve. Who of us has not become abruptly aware that we'd missed a key detail while taking the history of a patient because we'd been away in our own stories or so overwhelmed by our own personal plight that the plight of our patient faded in importance. Conversely, I believe that we all have known the joys of finding ourselves lost in the tales of our patients, having one precious moment of freedom from distraction with our own lives to be completely "in the moment" with a patient or client. We've all been in that place where our own life stories haven't mattered as much as the stories of our patients and when our minds were free from any distractions of time or task.

Showing up completely at the bedside, engaging our patients with the fullness of who we are, and being "in the moment" with them to our best ability involves being focused (mindfulness), attentive (awareness), and caring (compassionate). These three elements of minding the bedside bring us closer to the true nature of who we are, which is, genuinely caring individuals in touch with our most beneficent nature who wish to make a difference in the lives of those we attend to. It is these three elements, found within the discipline of many contemplation and meditation practices that we'll be discussing and practicing throughout this book.

Over the many years that I've been engaged in the nursing profession, what has become clear to me, time and again, is that in health care, *especially because of our charge to help others toward wholeness*, it benefits us as well as our patients if we've attained some degree of stability in our minds and if we're able to attend to the needs of another without losing our focus, attention, and compassion due to the stress or preoccupation of our own lives. Whether we're trying to help someone with depression find their way out of their dark underworld into the light of hope, helping a person recover from the dramatic (yet surprisingly routine) event of open-heart surgery, helping a new mother bring her newborn into the world, or trying to help someone have a good death, without being able to show up at the bedside with a mindful, aware, and compassionate presence, our sincere efforts are always incomplete, however small—or enormous—that incompleteness may be.

The way that we care for others and whether we can practice the elements of mindfulness (focus), meditative awareness (attention), and compassion (caring), may vary from one patient to another, or even from moment to moment. These key principles of a wakeful presence are what we work with as we enter into a practice of nursing from the heart of an awakened mind. And, as we work to develop them through a committed practice, we also find that they matter not only at the bedside, but—just as important—in our day-to-day lives as well.

What we stand to gain by strengthening our mindfulness and meditative awareness is a greater awareness of the present moments that we share with our patients and with the world. So if we ask, "Why should we practice meditation, why should we care about increasing our focus and attention?" the answer is simply that by doing so we engage our entire lives with a more present and aware state of being. And this kind of engagement brings us greater satisfaction and wisdom from all of the experiences that we encounter, whether those encounters are good and bad. Whether we're at the bedside working with our patients, having a dinner with our family, or undergoing our own medical procedure, being more present brings us more fully into each experience that we encounter.

A sense of abiding peace, or a discovery of a truer nature, is what we gradually come to realize as we gain stability in our mindfulness, meditative awareness, and compassionate presence. That abiding peace is what best serves our patients when we show up at the bedside. When we're able to communicate clearly, free from distractions, it helps our patients to embody that way of being too. And it's what best serves us, because it allows us to engage with the world in the most present manner and to appreciate all of life's circumstances as best we can.

What I grappled with in writing a book on mindfulness, meditative awareness, and compassion is that I have not arrived at a place in my life where I can remain completely mindful and aware (undistracted) while caring for another or even, for that matter, while driving in traffic. However, I reflected on a quote by Margaret Fuller, the 19th-century American journalist, critic, and women's rights advocate, who said, "If you have knowledge, let others light their candles at it." Following Fuller's example, I've begun to understand that while I am not completely free from distraction or unconditionally compassionate, I have been given the knowledge and tools that have helped me to work with my mind not only for the benefit of my patients, but for my own benefit as well. I've been practicing with these methods while engaged in my nursing practice for long enough to be able to share with you some of the things that have worked for me. So look at this book as a roadmap or as directions to a destination, one within your awakened heart and mind. Much as a sign points to a destination without being in that location, while I cannot know what is within your mind and heart, my role is to share with you some vital tools that have helped me and others like me deepen the connection with an awakened heart and to show up more fully present at the bedside. Let whatever light I may have gleaned from my personal experience with these practices at the bedside bring light to the journey that you have already undertaken by taking on the task of minding the bedside.

In writing this book, I am not implying that health-care practitioners lack the mindfulness or awareness to take care of their patients or that there is some wholesale deficit particular to health-care providers concerning compassion at the bedside. Far from it! Despite the enormous difficulties that can be encountered while delivering patient care—such as staffing issues, resource scarcity, and schedules jammed with a nonstop flow of patients—health-care practitioners do an incredible job of attending to the ills and woes of those they serve. I have worked with many individuals who have foregone all manner of personal comfort in deference to their patients and who work excruciatingly long hours and unreasonable shifts in order to provide compassionate care to those in need. These sacrifices are inspirational and filled with the best intentions of helping to alleviate suffering.

What is of concern is how we as nurses, as innately compassionate human beings, suffer due to our distraction from the present and how this distraction translates into the care we give others. Throughout our workdays, we lose focus, lose awareness, and lose the heart of our compassion due to our preoccupation and distraction. The suffering that comes with this kind of preoccupation and distraction is manifested in how we experience stress in our daily lives and how this stress takes us further away from our true nature in the moment. The unease that we feel when we are unable to meet the demands of those we care for in a compassionate manner is a profoundly negative addition to the stress that we already feel while working in the arena of health care.

The practices and discussions outlined in this book are about becoming more truly who we are, in *whatever we do*, without the constant distractions of thoughts and emotions that preoccupy our minds. Although I have written this book for an audience of health-care providers, the techniques presented here are not solely or simply for health-care practitioners. While the focus is on bringing mind and heart to the bedside, I believe that there is not one of us who cannot, in some way, learn to be more mindful, more aware, and more compassionate with our friends, our spouses, or our children; or to be more forgiving with those who annoy or anger us; or simply to be more compassionate with ourselves when we fail to live up to our own standards.

Through practicing mindfulness and meditative awareness and by cultivating a more genuine patient-centered approach that has as its basis a compassionate attention and focus, we can transform our activities of care at the bedside into a journey of personal transformation, utilizing the precious moments while engaged in our work as the path to increased happiness, self-awareness, and service. Looked at in this way, we have the potential to derive more benefit from our profession in whatever situation we find ourselves, engaging each fleeting moment as the opportunity to train ourselves in being present and caring with the world at large.

Because actually becoming mindful, aware, and compassionate can be a slow process and because cultivating an undistracted meditative awareness can take extensive practice, it's important to constantly remind ourselves that the times when we lack mindfulness and compassion are the most important lessons in learning how to practice. What we find as we're confronted with our lack of mindful compassion is that its opposite—mindful compassion—lies equally within our grasp. *Each moment of mindlessness is an invitation to become mindful.* Each lapse of awareness is a reminder to practice being aware. Each momentary and impermanent distraction within our mind, sometimes called an "arising," is a reminder of the impermanence of these distractions, the mental phenomena and perceptions that we experience. Each time that we find ourselves outside of the heart of the awakened mind of compassionate mindfulness, we are presented with the invitation to return to our unaltered mind, again and again, to return to our truer nature.

It is my task to convey the concepts and practices presented in this book in a coherent and sensible manner, in a way that honors their origin and brings them into relevance as they relate to the helping professions. Any truth that you find in the words that follow is not my truth; it is not any great achievement of my mind. The words, metaphors, and descriptions are derived directly from the teachings and practices of the many great teachers and scholars, from mystics, poets, and saints, and from the masters of the past and present who have given selflessly of their wisdom and experience.

Some of the discussions and examples that I share are direct teachings by these individuals, either in their words as noted or put into my own words in order that their meaning may be easily understood. Direct quotes as well as topics relevant to the discussion are noted as such and end-noted appropriately. If I have conveyed even a remote sense of their wisdom, it is only by their graces that I have been able to do so. Any failure to convey their wisdom is solely my lack of realization of these profound methods and should not be deemed a strike against any of the traditions, practices, or texts cited.

The exercises and practices that I present, while at times modified or personalized to meet the needs of this reading audience, find their roots in the timeless traditions of the world's contemplative and spiritual traditions. They should be used as practice exercises and are not necessarily the actual practices that the great contemplative and spiritual traditions have presented.

For specifics on the way to practice and for assistance in developing a schedule for practice, please turn to Appendix A, *How to Practice*, and to Appendix B, *Schedule for Practice*. There you will find the basic elements involved in the actual practice of mindfulness, meditative awareness, and compassion as well as an example of how to begin to schedule practice time into your day and advance the amount of time that you spend in formal practice.

After gaining some stability in doing these exercises, you may naturally find that there are some that work for you and others that don't; you may find that by modifying or changing the language, you are more able to relate to them and to make them yours. Wonderful! These techniques are a way for you to gain a familiarity with the kinds of meditative techniques that can lead to a deeper understanding of your heart and mind and are not the end-all in meditative practices.

As with any new disciple, practice is necessary. The only way to learn anything—whether it's the way that we practice nursing, speak French, raise children, or learn to race bicycles—is through practice. Mindfulness, meditation, and a compassionate presence are no different. What their embodiment requires of us is that we make a concerted effort to integrate them into our lives. We must become familiar enough with our mind when it isn't distracted and stable enough in our practice of these methods that we can engage with them after we've left our practice session and have entered into our daily lives.

If any of the words on these pages inspire you to deepen and more fully examine mindfulness and compassion, I encourage you to turn to the resource section in the back of this book and to visit my blog and website. There you will find the titles of works that have inspired me and others like me to pursue the path of mindfulness, meditation, and compassion. And should you find that you are moved to devote more of your time to studying these practices, I have listed various centers and teachers who are qualified to teach these practices, inspired by the realization of these methods.

Most of the individuals who I quote throughout this book have found their practice within the spiritual traditions. However, my intention is to bring a professional approach to mindfulness and compassion practices, not based on a specific faith or religious tradition. Still, because it is the spiritual and contemplative traditions that have been the source of wisdom from which I have derived the greatest benefit, I will use these sources as the basis for commentary and reference throughout the book.

While stories of saints and holy people provide the basis for emulation, and many of the world's contemplative practices flow from the spiritual traditions, the practices of mindfulness, meditative awareness, and compassion are inherently human abilities. Because the mind is universal in its dynamics and its attributes—particularly how distracted and altered it can become and, conversely, how it can be trained to a deeper level of realization—working with the mind is the realm of any motivated individual who wishes to wake up to his or her fuller potential.

My motivation for writing this book and for sharing these methods of working with the mind and cultivating compassion is no less than wishing that each one of you will find some jewel, some exercise or a few words, that will inspire you to a continued lifelong journey of practicing mindfulness, meditative awareness, and compassion, thereby deepening your connection with and your experience of your deepest nature. With this hope comes the inherent desire that, through these practices, you will also find your heart and mind *even more fully present* at the bedside and that, with this presence, your patients and clients will experience the benefits of these methods. May this be the case, and may the words in the following chapters inspire you in your art of caretaking.

A final note: within the development of this book, I may write something that appears not to be grounded in fact or that seems to be based upon supposition. As the discussion evolves, I hope to elaborate upon and cover all of the topics and concepts that I've introduced. If, by the end of the book, you're left with lingering questions or feel that I have erred in supporting premises that I've espoused, please visit my website and drop me a line. Please be specific about your feedback and about what you'd like more information on. I plan on updating and revising this book on an ongoing basis, and it is with your support that I'll succeed in providing you, the reader, with the best possible material on the subjects of mindfulness, meditative awareness, and compassion at the bedside. Thank you.

NOTE: The stories in this book are all true. Unless prior consent was given from those involved, most of the locations and names have been changed to protect anonymity. The essential versions have been minimally altered, although in each story I have created composite personae to protect the identities of individuals who would have otherwise been identifiable.

Chapter 1

Motivation

Each of us knows a genuine encounter from one based on deception. We've all been had at one time or another by people who seemed sincere in their intentions but whose motivations were insincere and who turned out to be deceitful. Conversely, we also know when we've been addressed honestly and respectfully; when someone, whether a loved one, a teacher or mentor, or even a patient, has seen within us our inherent goodness and that "self" that is beyond even our own perceived limitations.

In the same way, we also know when we're being genuine with our patients versus when we're showing up simply because we have to. When our motivation has been dampened by the hardships of our position or by the strain of compassion fatigue, when we're not showing up at the bedside fully present, we fail ourselves in what is our most selfless potential. Instead of seeing our patients with a mind free from distractions and remaining present and undistracted, we glance at the wall clock, ruffle through the chart, carry out our planned intervention, and beat a hasty retreat for the door.

Our patients sense when we're showing up at the bedside and when we're not, though they may not directly express it to us. Because our intention and motivations can have a direct impact on our patients' well-being[1],[2] it is imperative that we check our motivation every time we engage with our patients… or really anyone, for that matter!! By making our primary motivation to be of service and to create a healing relationship no matter what barriers exist, we instill each encounter with a focused, attentive, and heartfelt presence that can transcend all manner of difficulties and obstacles.

> When…[one]…walks into a room with a patient…[one's] true attitude toward the patient will be immediately visible, regardless of the attitude that…[one]…attempts to portray. Something intangible is revealed that reflects…[one's]… actual motivation or attitude. The caring motivation needs to be genuine, because it is perceived by the patient. It can't

be faked.³ *(In this quote, I've inserted "one" in the place of "a doctor(s)" to note that this applies to anyone within the health-care profession.)*

The training in mindfulness (focus), meditative awareness (attention), and compassion (caring) has within its heart the greatest benefit when the intention for doing so comes from the true motivation to *change oneself for the benefit of others*. This point cannot be stressed too much or too often: our motivation to work with our mind has the greatest benefit when the heart of that motivation is to *change how we are for the benefit of others*. This way of thinking, of benefiting others through working on oneself, can become a powerful motivator for change, especially when we come up against our limitations. Changing ourselves for the benefit of others can be an invigorating and refreshing motivator in the struggles that we encounter as we begin our work on becoming less distracted and more compassionate. Instead of isolating ourselves in the process, our motivation for continuing on the path can be infused with the spirit of doing so for the benefit of our family, friends, and patients. The Dalai Lama describes this as a "wise selfishness," whereby the work that we do in our own self-interest can benefit others in its results.

For myself, I know that whenever my mind is too far from where it ought to be, if I can bring myself back to the primary motivation of working to change myself for the benefit of another, then it can transform how I am and the quality of my moment-to-moment awareness and presence. This kind of transformation of one's awareness, repeated again and again over the course of a work shift, can be the antidote to feeling burned out at the bedside and can infuse one's work with a vital intent on bringing care and compassion into patients' lives.

In learning to become more mindful, aware, and compassionate, it's vital to use *all of our interactions* with our patients and clients as opportunities to reaffirm our motivation and to practice mindfulness and compassion. We are presented daily with numerous opportunities to see what it is that motivates us in our profession. If we get into the habit of ignoring certain situations that we find particularly challenging, believing that we can't possibly change our perceptions or reactions to them, then it will be impossible for us to change our motivation and to remain mindfully aware and compassionate when difficulties arise. As long as we give a "special exemption" status to particular situations, for example when a patient is combative or noncompliant, then it will be difficult to fine-tune our mind's way of relating to the world. When we accept any and all situations as invitations to practice being our most mindful and most compassionate self, then no matter the hardship, we can face anything knowing that what we are doing is furthering our progress on the path and we can "participate joyfully in the sorrows of the world."[4]

It's fair to assume that our motivation for being in health care is, for the most part, rooted in the heart of caring for another. Whether our vocational decision has also been informed by consideration of monetary gains, flexibility in the type of work that we do, a sense of duty, or any number of views, when working with those in need or who are suffering, we all have a basic concern for our patients' and clients' well-being. In the course of our career or even within the course of one shift, our motivation will vary; we may be unenthused with a particular rotation, assignment, or patient, or we may be tired or challenged by our own personal circumstances. We may have lost our initial idealism due to years of thankless shift work. Whatever the reasons and motivations, it's vital that we reaffirm an attentive and caring practice on a daily basis.

I remember a peer of mine saying that each time she arrived at work, before she went in the door, she breathed a sigh of resignation at having to go into a thankless job once again. I thought about that statement and shortly thereafter began breathing out a strong breath of determination just before I entered the door that whatever I did, I would do wholeheartedly and with the intention of helping all those who I worked with, patients as well as peers. Not only did this seem to shift my perceptions and my negative attitudes at work, but when I shared this idea with the peer who had verbalized her resignation, she delighted in the idea and soon began to change her attitude in how she showed up at work as well. I also began to use this one-breath-meditation frequently throughout the shift and found that it helped me stay more focused and attentive in the most pressing of situations.

Throughout this book, you'll encounter passages in **this font**. These passages will either be exercises, reminders, or opportunities to reflect on the current discussion. Treat the exercises as moments to practice the principles and topics of discussion, putting the book down as time allows, trying out the method or methods being discussed. Treat these moments as a time out for your mind.

> Before you enter your workplace or when you come home from work, take a deep breath, reaffirm your reason for being where you are, and breath out any resistance to being there. Reaffirm your commitment to providing the most present, undistracted, attentive, and compassionate self to your patients,

your peers, your family, and your friends. And then,
just let it all go.

If we reflect on it for even a moment, we can see that our motivation is most altruistic when it emanates from a place of genuine, compassionate, and mindful caring, from a place of unconditional positive regard for another, with a sense that that person matters just as much as we do. When we connect from a place of compassion, *born not out of pity* but out of the realization that the other person—like us—wishes to be happy and free from suffering, the end result will be evident in how our patients experience us, regardless of other pressures or other motivating factors. They'll get the sense that our motivation is to do whatever we can, including remaining undistracted, to make their outcome a more positive one.

The kind of motivation that we're working on here is a deep and abiding respect for another's suffering and a conviction and desire to do whatever it takes to alleviate that person's suffering…even if doing so seems impossible!

In defining *compassion*, which we'll discuss in more depth in Chapter 4 of this book, Sogyal Rinpoche writes,

> What is compassion? It is not simply a sense of sympathy or caring for the person suffering, not simply a warmth of heart toward the person before you, or a sharp clarity of recognition of their needs and pain; it is also a sustained and practical determination to do whatever is possible and necessary to help alleviate their suffering.[5]

When our motivation is "a sustained and practical determination to do whatever is possible," then laxity of purpose and burnout have a more difficult time enticing us with their promise of ease and apathy.

Tempering our motivation comes slowly and is sustained by an ongoing reaffirmation of that motivation. When we get out of bed in the morning, while eating, before entering the door to work, while walking the halls on rounds—in every moment we are offered the opportunity to reestablish our motivation and intention for our presence in the healing environment. By investigating our intentions and motivation at the bedside, catching ourselves in the act of checking out as well as finding ourselves showing up, we gain a deeper glimpse into our truer nature, the union of our heart and mind that finds as its primary motivation the alleviation of suffering.

For a moment, reflect on times in your life when you felt a sense of motivation based on altruism and compassion, when thoughts of duty, pride, and responsibility faded into the generous mind of some greater good. Focus on the moments when you had "a sustained and practical determination to do whatever...[was]...possible." Focus on those moments that might have moved you, even surprised you; when your concern with yourself lessened and your determination to help another was primary. Think of the times when the outcome of the moment wasn't linked with how your professional image would or wouldn't be viewed. How did it feel? What didn't you feel in terms of anxiety, pressure, and time constraints?

> Try taking "motivation breaks" throughout the day. Just stop. Remember why you're here. Imagine yourself at your very best. What is your motivation for being at the bedside?

We may find that as we begin to reflect on motivation and intention, our mind wants to shift to a motivation based on an altruistic impulse. In this way, we can affirm the inherently compassionate nature that is the basis of our decision to care for others. The more that we can reflect on our motivation and strengthen it through mindfulness, meditative awareness, and compassionate practices, the more we will contradict the less-than-altruistic impulses that arise in our daily encounters. It is through the ongoing and repeated shifting of one's motivation that one begins to attend mindfully and compassionately toward those one is serving.

One major benefit that may result from our reestablishing our motivation continually throughout the day is that doing so can work as a powerful antidote to the fatigue and burnout that can occur when we're working in a less-than-idyllic environment or when we're overly taxed due to work-related stress. By constantly reaffirming our motivation, coming back to a mindful understanding of our intention, we can contradict the transient negative thought patterns and emotions that occur when we're compassion-fatigued. So, whenever we find ourselves wondering why we went into our profession, establishing a *compassionate motivation* helps remind our mind of its goodness. It may also help us to get out of a routine of less-than-beneficial thinking that we may have become entrenched in.

Throughout the remainder of this book and while doing the exercises that are presented, you may wish to establish your motivations for working with yourself by using some statement of affirmation. There are many ways of doing this. One method is simply to recite a few lines or a verse from something that inspires you, perhaps a phrase or lines of a poem. You can think, or say quietly, "May everyone I work with today be greeted by my best self," or, "May I remember that my patients are suffering and that they want to be happy just like I do." It's not necessary to make an elaborate motivation; anything that can help you to connect with your most positive reasons for helping others will do.

You also may wish to create a more elaborate motivation, where you include different aspects of what it would be like to care completely from an awakened heart. One such verse that I use and that I've modified for the context of working with patients goes something like:

> By the power and the truth of my fundamental goodness,
> May all those I work with have happiness and its causes,
> May they be free from suffering and its causes,
> May they never be separated from this happiness, devoid of suffering
> And may they remain in a state of equanimity, free from all attachment and aversion

This is just one verse. There are infinite ways for you to establish your motivation. In this case, the affirmation that it is my fundamental goodness that is at work reminds me to not get caught up with the distractions that can arise in my mind. By wishing that all those I work with will have happiness and its causes, I'm also wishing for them that they too can rely on their fundamental goodness. By wishing that they be free from suffering, I'm essentially wishing for them what I'm wishing for myself—a recognition of a greater self that can deal with life and so lessen the effects of adversity. Wishing that they never be separated from this happiness is also what I wish for myself, that I can remain in this undistracted and compassionate presence. And finally, wishing that they remain in a state of equanimity is wishing that the thoughts and emotions that do arise in their minds will not prevent them from finding their own inner peace and happiness. Whenever I focus on these lines and put their words into practice, I see a difference in how I attend to others, whether the other is my wife, my friend, a homeless person on the street, or a patient at the bedside.

Summary and Reminders:

1. Our patients sense when we're showing up at the bedside and when we're not.

2. By setting our motivation first, to be of service and to create a healing relationship no matter what barriers exist, we instill each encounter with a heartfelt presence that can transcend all manner of difficulties and obstacles.

3. The training in mindfulness, meditative awareness, and compassion has within its heart the greatest grace when its impulse emanates from the true motivation to *change oneself for the benefit of others*.

4. In learning to become more mindfully compassionate, it's vital to use all of our interactions with our patients and clients as clarifiers of our motivation.

5. Tempering our motivation comes slowly and is sustained by an ongoing reaffirmation of that motivation.

6. By investigating our intentions and motivation at the bedside, catching ourselves in the act of checking out as well as finding ourselves showing up, we gain a deeper glimpse into our truer nature.

7. One major benefit that may result from our reestablishing our motivation continually throughout the day is that it can work as a powerful antidote to the fatigue and burnout that can settle in when we're working in a less-than-idyllic environment or when we're taxed due to work-related stress.

8. Throughout the day, whether at work or home, use brief motivational exercises to reaffirm what is inherently compassionate about your choice to help others.

Chapter 2

Riding the Breath to the Meditative Mind

One of the basic tenets of meditation is the notion that passive awareness is a natural, elementary, and direct form of experience that is ordinarily overwhelmed and obscured by the activity of the mind. The purpose of meditation, therefore, is to allow the mind to become quiet and thereby uncover the capacity for this experience.[6]

—Marjorie Schuman, from *The Psychobiology of Consciousness*

Mindfulness and meditative awareness are about learning to know our minds well enough to be able to interrupt our preoccupation with the ongoing stream of thoughts and emotions that normally run our lives, releasing all of our cares into the undistracted and natural simplicity of the true nature of our own minds. In this case, the term *natural simplicity* refers to the ability to release ourselves from the preoccupation of thoughts that the mind normally engages in. We'll discuss this again later in the book.

It is within this natural simplicity—the undistracted mind—that we actually come to find or know parts of ourselves that we'd only had glimpses of in the past. And what we find is a self that is much more spacious, more compassionate, and more insightful than any self we have known. It is this self that, when presented at the bedside, has the greatest potential for healing our patients and clients. It is this genuine self that presents itself when one loses one's preoccupation with oneself in favor of a mindful and compassionate presence with one's patient.

I'm using two terms here—*mindfulness* and *meditative awareness*—which I'll elaborate on here along with *meditation*. For now, think of mindfulness as focus, as an aspect of attending to the present whereby we attend to some "thing"—the breath, the moment, the story of a patient. It is an open and spacious focus, not a focus where we furrow our brow and try to intensely do "something," whereby we anchor our attention and know that our focus is on some "thing"—the breath, our patient, etc. It is an aspect of a compassionate presence, one without which we cannot fully engage in a present attentiveness to our patient.

Meditative awareness is attention; it's the awareness that we have when we know that we are focusing on or remaining mindful of something. It is the "watcher" or overseer that knows we're being mindful and that brings us back to the present moment when we become distracted. It is being aware that we're mindful, alert to the moment and to the fact that we're focused yet relaxed without grasping onto the object of our focus. Also, awareness is *the most important factor* in preventing us from becoming distracted.

Finally, meditation—as we'll discuss it here and later in the book—relates to a state where we simply *are* in the present, attending to the present, in an undistracted state of mind, of being. It is actually a state of nondoing, where there is not the slightest effort made to "be meditating," where the present moment isn't based on the thought that we should be meditating or doing anything. We "simply be." While this way of being may sound far-fetched or may seem unrealistic for us at the present, varying levels of this way of being—mindful and aware—are accessible to us here, right now.

Again, from *The Tibetan Book of Living and Dying*, Sogyal Rinpoche writes:

> To meditate is to make a complete break with how we "normally" operate, for it is a state free of all cares and concerns, in which there is no competition, no desire to possess or grasp at anything, no intense and anxious struggle, and no hunger to achieve: an ambitionless state where there is neither acceptance nor rejection, neither hope nor fear, a state in which we slowly begin to release all those emotions and concepts that have imprisoned us, into the space of natural simplicity.[7]

The state of simply being is a state free of any "thing"; a state free from all "cares and concerns" and from all opposites, or duality, where we don't get caught up in the normal way of thinking "I don't like this thought...I do like that thought." It's a way of being whereby we allow more spaciousness in who and how we are by allowing our mind to simply "be" without worrying about what thoughts or emotions are arising within it.

When we think of this kind of meditation, especially as it relates to the art of caretaking, the essential quality of this kind of practice is being able to be completely present and undistracted, "meditative," with our patients and clients. It is the ability to remain free from the distractions of our own mind to attend instead to the mind of the "other." It's almost as if, when we are engaged to this depth with another, we cease to "be," at least in terms of our distraction by the constant chatter that permeates our ordinary mind. Instead, there is a quality of selflessness that simply "exists," almost unbidden, that we "drop into," when we're genuinely attending to another.

As health-care practitioners, at one time or another we've probably found ourselves in the state of "simply being," perhaps even unintentionally. Maybe we've even stumbled into a mental state where we've lost the self-referential quality of conversation, not thinking about ourselves, and have become completely immersed, selfless, in the situation and story of our patient. Perhaps we've allowed ourselves, for the moment, to take a break from our routine and in the interest of a moment of sanity have fully immersed ourselves in really being present with the person in front of us. And if we've not been fortunate enough to have this happen in our professional lives, then perhaps in other parts of our lives—when tending to our children, making love with our partner, when experiencing the artistic arrest that comes with viewing great works of creativity or listening to great pieces of music. At some point we've all experienced what some would call the transcendent, the divine, deeper nature of our minds.

What we've experienced during these moments are gaps or spaces in the ways that we normally perceive and experience things. Space from our mundane, worried, preoccupied, judging, analyzing, frenzied, and exhausted mind! What meditative awareness and mindfulness are then—in simple terms—are skillful methods of prolonging these gaps or spaces in our normal way of thinking, allowing us to remain undistracted and slowing the return to the discursive or "chatty" mind.

The gaps that we experience during moments of presence are prolonged when we slow our habitual distraction of following the thoughts that arise within our minds, when we bring our minds home instead of allowing them to jump from one distracting thought to another. It's not so much that we need to control the thoughts, emotions, and sensations that occur, because it isn't these "mind dynamics" that are the problem any more than the clouds in the sky are problems to the sky. The challenge is our tendency to follow these mental phenomena rather than to rest in the gaps in between them or to enjoy the "space" that can open up when we aren't preoccupied with thinking. What we're more used to is the habitual pattern of missing the moment due to getting lost in thoughts about the past or thinking too much about the future instead of resting in the present.

Imagine that we are sitting with a good friend, a family member, or a loved one outside on a glorious day. The sun is shining and there is not a cloud in sight. The breeze blows around our face, cooling us just enough to get a flavor, a taste, of the air. Completely in the moment, all cares ceased, not a single distraction remains in our minds. We are completely sharing the moment, aware of the other's presence, not sidetracked by thoughts of what has been or what we have to do later. All of a sudden, a cloud blocks the sun, the air darkens and cools, the breeze picks up, and our skin chills ever so slightly. The tranquility of the moment is broken, and we become distracted by the changes. Now, instead of focusing on the moment as it is, we become preoccupied with these changes. We look into the sky to find more clouds following the one that has obscured the sun, and we become totally distracted from the moment. We begin to imagine what will happen when more clouds come and what we've done in the past when clouds or even rain have come. After about 10 minutes of being distracted, we suddenly realize that the other person that we were with has gotten up and left some time ago. Where they were once sitting is a note saying, "Nice spending some time with you; let's do it again when you're not so distracted."

To a great extent, this is how we are with our own minds, getting lost in some momentary "cloudiness of thought" instead of remaining attentive to the present moment. At one moment we're enjoying the presence of the moment, while in the next moment, we're distracted by some cloud arising in our consciousness and have lost the immediacy of the moment. What we need, then, is a method for bringing our minds back, bringing our focus back to the present and, at the bedside, back to our patient.

Right now, without even trying, without even thinking about it, we're breathing. Yet we rarely think about our breath or even take time to notice that we are in fact breathing. It's just one of those natural things that we do that goes by completely unnoticed unless, of course, we're diagnosed with a respiratory illness, have a pulmonary pathology, are dying, or—as in the following example—are subjected to the loss of our breathing for any amount of time.

A meditation instructor and her student were sitting by the banks of a gently flowing river, with the student receiving instructions on how to mindfully watch the breath. After some time of watching her breath, the student interrupted her instructor, saying, "I don't know what you find particularly interesting about the breath," whereupon her instructor grabbed the student by the scruff of the neck and held her head under the water for a period of 30 seconds. Gasping for breath when she was finally released, the student screamed at her instructor, "Why the hell did you do that?? I could have died!!" The instructor smiled and calmly answered, "And did you find your breath interesting then?"

> Just for a moment, become aware of your breath. Simply notice your breathing. There's no need to change how you're breathing, just breathe. Interesting, isn't it? You go on breathing without ever having to try to breathe, without needing to be aware of it. The same is true with your mind; without "thinking" about it, your mind goes on thinking about thoughts, getting caught up in what it's thinking about, and creating stories about the stories that come and go like the clouds in the sky.

We begin to learn mindfulness and meditation by observing our breath because it is always there, because we can do it anywhere—in the car at a red light, on a plane, as we're going to sleep, when we're stressed out at work… even when we're dying. It's an easily available anchor to which we can repeatedly return when we notice that our mind is distracted, something that we can become familiar with as we start to practice the art of mindfully watching the present. And, as we become more skilled in observing our own breath, we can help our patients with their challenges by helping them to do the same.[8]

Without our necessarily being conscious of it, our breath changes all the time depending upon the state of our mind. On an obvious level, this occurs, for instance, when we're anxious or excited; our breathing becomes faster. On a more subtle level we notice that when we're tense, we may hold our breath without even knowing it; or when we're depressed, our breath may become shallow. In this way, the mind rides on the breath, and it is through learning to observe the breath that we begin to learn to watch the mind.

In beginning to meditate, *all we're doing is watching the breath, not altering or modifying it.* By learning to simply observe the breath, we can learn to use it as an *anchor for our attention.* By mindfully attending to our breath, we begin to become aware of the present breath, without changing it, without trying to alter it. In the same way, as we progress, we'll learn to do this with our thoughts, emotions, and bodily sensations, simply observing them without getting caught up in a story about them, without trying to change them. Eventually, we can arrive in the present moment with the same attentiveness—watching, observing, not judging…simply being.

Next we're going to work with an exercise for watching the breath. After reading the following script or, if it applies, listening to the audio track, just put the book down and practice the exercise for a few minutes. Whatever happens, use your breath as the anchor of your attention. When you get distracted, bring it back to the breath. When you become dull, happy, anxious, bored, elated… wherever you find your mind, bring your attention back to the breath.

Set aside all cares about what you're going to do next, where you may need to be, or—if you're doing this at night—whether you're going to fall asleep before you finish this exercise. If you have something that you must get to now, then come back to this section when you have the time to be present with this material.

If you're at work and have the time and ability to set aside 15 minutes, you may find that doing this exercise during your shift can help strengthen your mindfulness at work and throughout the day. Read the following script normally, in an unhurried manner, taking time to read it slowly, pausing between lines, taking care to read each line as an exercise in presence of mind. The difference here is that you're using the words as a cue to watch your breath. Read. Breath. Read. Breath. Yeah, like that. If you'd like, you may download an audio copy of this exercise from my website at www.mindingthebedside.com. Or, if you need a CD of all of the tracks used in this book, please go to my website and request a free copy of the CD, I'd be happy to send one to you. This exercise is listed as "Track #1: Riding the Breath."

> Sitting on a straight-backed chair or couch or on a cushion on the floor, allow your body to become still. The back is straight without being stiff; the posture is relaxed, awake, and dignified. The hands can rest gently on the knees or in the lap. The eyes are open, simply resting the gaze on whatever is in front of you, without thinking too much about what you're viewing. Settling into this moment, begin watching the breath.
>
> Become aware of the fact that you're breathing. Become aware of the movement of the breath as it flows into and out of the body. Feel the breath as it comes into the body and as it leaves the body. Simply remain aware of the breath flowing in and flowing out, not manipulating the breathing in any way. Simply being aware of it and noticing how it feels.

When your mind becomes distracted—and it will become distracted—simply return to the breath. No commentary. No judgment.

Allow yourself to be with this flow of breath, coming in and going out. Notice the feeling of the breath as the lungs fill with air on the in-breath and deflate as you breathe out, the chest expanding and collapsing. Perhaps feeling the breath in the abdomen, rising as you breathe in and flattening and sinking as you breathe out. Allow your attention to gently ride on the sensation of each breath, not thinking about breathing, without the need to comment. Simply watching your breathing.

Allow the breath to naturally breathe itself, not needing to change it in any way, giving full attention to each breath. Observe the full cycle of each breath, locating the very beginning of the breath, as it enters the nose or mouth, and following it as it fills the lungs and expands the chest and the abdomen, then comes to the gap where there is neither in-breath nor out-breath, before it turns around and makes its journey out of the body. Simply remain present for the cycle of each breath, being there, letting your attention gently float on the awareness of your breath.

After a short time, you may notice that the mind wanders off to thoughts of the past, fantasies, memories, or regrets. Or it may move to anticipation of the future, planning, wishing, and judging. You may find yourself thinking about what you'll do after this exercise, what you have to do at work, things that you have to do.

As soon as you become aware that the attention has moved off the breath, guide it back to the next breath with a gentle and firm awareness.

There's no need to give yourself a hard time, saying, "How did I become so distracted?" Simply come back to this breath. Watching the breath and the arising thoughts without judgment, simply observing. Once again, bringing the attention to this breath, in this moment. Breathing in with the in-breath, breathing out with the out-breath. Feeling the movement in your body. The breath anchoring the attention in this moment.

When the mind wanders, bring your attention back to the breath, knowing that you can always use the awareness of your breath to refocus your attention, to return to the present. Whenever you notice that you have drifted from the present—when you become distracted, preoccupied, or restless—the attention on the breath can be a powerful anchor to this moment and to this state of awake stillness.

And now, for the time remaining, let go of all particular objects of attention, allowing yourself to simply be here, simply present. Breath moving, sensations in the body, sounds, thoughts, all of it coming and going...allowing all of it...and dropping into being, into stillness, present with it all, as it unfolds, complete, as you are, whole.

And...relax.

What you may have noticed was that your attention was everywhere but on the breath; that you were able to keep your attention on the breath for a few breaths, if that, and then you were off again into daydreams, thoughts, and concerns. That's perfectly fine, because that's what is going on all the time in our minds. The purpose of this exercise is to introduce us to our minds, to our everyday minds, to the minds that we will be working with as we learn the practices of a mindful, aware, and compassionate presence, and part of getting to know our mind is getting to know how distracted—or not—it can be.

Remembering that mindfulness is the focus on the breath and that awareness in knowing when we've become distracted from this focus, simply use this exercise as a method to train in mindfulness and awareness. At this point in time, it's not as important that we are able to watch our breath as it is that we are able to begin to recognize when we've become distracted. Because we tend to become easily distracted without even noticing that we've done so, it's important for us to take as much time as we need to become acquainted with our minds and to become accustomed to an almost unacknowledged habit of being everywhere at once.

The purpose of mindfulness *is not to learn how to watch our breath.* We simply use watching the breath as a way to anchor our attention. An important note belongs here: What I've found in the mindfulness classes that I've taught is that many people use the breath *as a distraction rather than as an anchor.* Oftentimes, when I ask people how they're doing, they'll say, "Great!" When I begin to inquire more deeply, I find that what these people are doing is using the breath as the source for more inner dialogue. Instead of simply resting with the mind focused on the breath, people begin to make up stories and distractions about the breath. Instead of simply watching the breath, as an observer, people tend to watch the breath as if they were commenting on a tennis match, "Breath in, breath out, breath in, breath out."

Three weeks into a class that I was teaching, after bringing up this point, one perplexed woman said, "You mean that we're not supposed to be saying to ourselves, 'Now I'm breathing in, now I'm breathing out?' Then what are we supposed to be doing, nothing?" Exactly! Well, kind of. We actively observe the breath, as it is, without commenting on it. We focus on the breath and become aware of the fact that we've become distracted from the breath, bringing our attention repeatedly back to the breath. So we aren't simply zoning out, spacing out, getting lost in space. We're keeping the attention focused on the breathing as an anchor, while the mind remains clear, using awareness to bring the focus back to the moment when we realize that we've become distracted.

Doing *just this and no more*, being this way, takes time. It takes practice. It takes patience. It takes a meditative awareness. And *it takes being very forgiving and compassionate with ourselves.* The lessons in patience with ourselves and the awareness, compassion, and resulting stability of the mind that we gain as we practice will naturally flow out to others as we learn to embody it within ourselves. When we become less distracted, then our attention to the world is more present.

Meditation starts out as the formal practice that we begin with to become more present at the bedside, and it includes not only the components of mindfulness and awareness but spaciousness as well. From our last exercise, we can begin to understand what these components entail: *mindfully* remaining in the present, *aware* when we've been distracted, and *spaciously* returning, again and again, to our moment to moment awareness, not squeezing our attention too much in an attempt to observe the breath. We'll come back to these three dynamics of attending to the present in Chapter 6; for now, we'll focus on mindfulness.

What we find when we begin to meditate is that it's much more difficult than we might've imagined. Meditation requires practice, patience, and persistence. Sogyal Rinpoche writes:

> Just as a writer learns the spontaneous freedom of expression only after years of often grueling study, and just as the simple grace of a dancer is achieved only with enormous, patient effort, so when you begin to understand where meditation will lead you, you will approach it as the greatest endeavor of your life, one that demands of you the deepest perseverance, enthusiasm, intelligence, and discipline.[9]

How do we maintain the "deepest perseverance, enthusiasm, intelligence, and discipline" necessary to develop a deep and abiding mindfulness? First, we check our motivation and realize, over and over again, that our ability to be of the most benefit to everyone we work or deal with demands of us a focused, attentive, and compassionate presence based on the motivation to be present for their benefit. Without really understanding the absolute imperative that demands of us a clear and undistracted mind, we are liable to fall back into a mindless way of doing things. Hence, we strengthen the skills of mindfulness, meditative awareness, and compassion through the practice of consistent meditation—on a day-to-day basis, if possible—to establish an unshakable stability of mind. Additionally, in terms of long-term benefits, by practicing these techniques, we ultimately benefit ourselves in every part of our lives, not just at work. Finally, after consistently attending to our minds and becoming adept at bringing our minds home and bringing our attention to the present, we'll begin to experience a certain dysphoria if we neglect our practice. We'll actually look forward to our "timeouts," and we'll become hopelessly addicted to becoming more clear—what an addiction!!

> So, once again, just...simply...watch your breath. Perhaps put this book down, sit in an alert and relaxed position, and simply train your focus on the breath...allow the attention to ride the breath. And, if you become distracted, come back to the breath. Again. And again.
>
> After a few minutes, just relax. Drop all methods. And just be.

Summary and Reminders:

1.   Mindfulness and meditative awareness are about learning to know our minds well enough to be able to interrupt our grasping at the ongoing stream of thoughts and emotions that normally run our lives.

2.   It is within this natural simplicity of the mind that we actually come to find or know parts of ourselves that we've only had glimpses of in the past.

3.   Think of mindfulness as an aspect of attending to the present whereby we attend to some thing—the breath, the moment, the story of a patient, etc.

4.   Meditative awareness is the process whereby we know that we are remaining mindful of something or of some process.

5.   Meditative awareness and mindfulness are skillful methods of prolonging the gaps in our normal stream of thoughts, of learning to remain undistracted and slow the return to the discursive mind.

6.   We begin to learn mindfulness by observing our breath because it is always there, because we can do it anywhere.

7.   The purpose of mindfulness *is not to learn how to watch our breath.* We simply use watching the breath as a way to anchor our attention.

8.   Refer to Appendix A, *How to Practice*, for an explanation of the important elements of formal practice.

9.   Refer to Appendix B, *Schedule for Practice*, and begin with Week 1 (unless you wish to increase the amount of time that you spend).

10. You may wish to go to my website at www.mindingthebedside.com to download guided meditation tracks, MP3s, and other tools that will help facilitate your practice. Again, if you need to, you may also go to my website to order a free copy of a CD with all of the tracks used in this book.

Chapter 3

Who's Minding the Bedside?

I'm stuck in Washington at Dulles Airport's *G* terminal with several hundred other souls crammed into the boarding area. Outside, flashes of lightning illuminate the cloud-darkened sky. The loud thunderclap strikes come alarmingly close to this small, overcrowded weigh station. As we watch the *Departure* boards, one flight after another posts *CANCELED*, and a tide of anxious and angry passengers washes over the customer-service desk, employees frightened for their well-being. How appropriate it is, then, that I am on my way back from teaching a class on mindfulness to a group of health-care practitioners in Seattle. What a better way for me to practice what I've been preaching.

—From a journal entry made by the author some years ago

That night in Terminal G, as each cancellation was posted on the board, I heard a rumble of comments such as, "If this doesn't change, I'm going to have to strangle someone!," "..I can't believe that this is happening!" and "what's wrong with them?!" I wondered who the "them" was that this poor distraught woman was angry with? How could "they" control the ability of airplanes to fly through massive summer thunderstorms?

We've all known the kind of frustration that arises when something beyond our control occurs. Unable to control the thoughts that arise in our mind and the emotions that ripple through our body, we look for someone or something "out there" to blame for the way that we're feeling. Sometimes there really is a "they" who seem, in some way or another, partially to blame for our circumstances. But, are they to blame for our state of mind? Is it they who have actually caused the eruption of stress hormones coursing through our veins? Is it they who have brought the furrowed brow, the sweaty palms, the cascade of catecholamines? Or…is it "we," "me," "I" who try desperately to blame something on forces external to ourselves so that we won't feel so powerless?

The recognition that we can't change the weather gives us the opportunity to change our relationship with it by accepting that the clouds and storms are simply part of the landscape, dynamics of the sky. In the same way, when we decide to work with the thoughts and emotions that arise in our minds, realizing that they are like the clouds in the sky—temporary and transient—then we can intimately change our relationship to this "cloudiness" and in how we relate to and perceive what arises. We can learn to watch our thoughts and, instead of canceling our rendezvous with the present, we can remove our obsessive focus on the "clouds," seeing instead the brilliance of our undistracted sky-like mind behind the clouds. When we begin to see what arises in our mind as simple dynamic phenomena within the environment of our mind, just as clouds are phenomena of the environment of the sky, then we can begin to take them less seriously.

The habit of turning the mind toward trying to change the outer circumstances frequently happens when one falls ill or is given a diagnosis that threatens one's sense of "self." Unable to deal with the enormity of the emotions and feelings that arise around having an illness, a person may strike out at anyone within range, attempting to alleviate the feelings of powerlessness, somehow hoping that by gaining control over their external environment, they'll find peace internally.

Within the health-care setting, nurses and physicians are the closest targets of a patient's raw emotions, but the recipient of this outwardly projected frustration can be anyone who comes within range of a mind left unattended, obscured by intense emotional turmoil. Anyone walking into the room—a nurse, physician, social worker, or relative (and sometimes especially so)—can be the target of others' attempts at alleviating their inner suffering by changing the outer environment.

The storm clouds of illness can be immense, particularly if the illness is life-threatening or life-altering. The dark thunderheads of emotions can obscure even the brightest rays of hope and the bluest skies of the future, leaving a darkened landscape drenched with the downpour of sorrow and suffering. The lightning strikes of anger and frustration that the patient directs towards a health-care provider can be devastating to those who, in their hearts, have chosen caregiving as a profession out of a compassionate impulse.

While we may not be able to change the force of the emotional lightning strike, we can use the lightning rod of a mind rooted in mindfulness, meditative awareness, and compassion to transform the power of such outbursts into the very cause of change within our own minds. If we can ground another's emotional distress through the heart of our own self-concern, that part of us that takes another's sorrow personally, and realize that this person's outbursts have very little to do with who we really are, we can redefine who we are in relation to our reactions to these stressors. To do this, we need to begin taming our mind and to work with our tendencies to dwell on the mental phenomena that arise—our reactions, judgments, and perceptions; we need to transform how our mind deals with the "arisings" or phenomena that appear like clouds in the sky. The transformation that makes this possible is when we begin to realize that who is showing up at the bedside (or at home, or in traffic) is not just our feelings or our thoughts.

> Just for a moment, recall a time when you were blamed for something that you didn't do, or a time when someone dumped their emotional baggage on you for something that you had done, and you took it personally. It can be anyone—a patient, peer, perhaps your spouse, parent, or child. Feel into it, physically and psychologically. Pause.
>
> Have you ever felt so victimized by someone else's "stuff" that you just felt like screaming at them or hitting them? Feel that feeling now. Really bring into your mind the thoughts that occurred. Pause.
>
> Allow your physiology to be with that moment, and allow your body to feel how it felt then.
>
> Did you find yourself ruminating on the other person's faults? Did you have to suppress your own reactions? Bring up the thoughts that surrounded this event clearly in your mind.
>
> For a brief moment, revisit the feelings of discomfort that accompany your memory of this event, and relive in your body and mind what it felt like. Allow that discomfort to reside, ever so briefly, within your physiology. If you can do this, continue with it for about a minute. Then, just let it all go and come back to the present.

In this short exercise, when you revisited this event, who showed up in this situation, and is that the same person who is reading this book right now? If we are not our thoughts, our emotions, or our memories, then *are we* or *how are we* the same person who we were when this event occurred? It's amazing, really, that even though we are constantly changing, although our thoughts about ourselves change from moment to moment, *we tend to attach meaning to the thoughts and emotions that we experience when we just remember an event that was hard for us.* We identify so strongly with our thoughts and emotions, and with the stories that we make up in our minds, that we not only believe them to be the truth but end up becoming them!

Minding the bedside mindfully, aware, and compassionately comes from realizing the changing nature of our thoughts and from turning and returning the mind inward, transforming the stormy arisings of thoughts, emotions, and feelings and recognizing them to be impermanent phenomena like passing clouds in the sky. Minding the bedside comes from realizing that whatever thoughts and emotions may be stirred up while doing our job are simply the result of our past experiences and attitudes and have very little to do with the present moment. And it's the same for our patients too!

The nature of clouds is to arrive, float within the sky for a while, and then leave. The nature of the sky is to remain spacious, open, and present, regardless of whether a storm cloud or rainbow appears in front of it. To paraphrase a saying, the sky is neither perturbed when clouds pass through it, nor particularly flattered when a rainbow appears.

In the very same way, when observed mindfully with awareness, our thoughts, whether "good" or "bad," will simply pass through our mind and then dissipate and disappear...if allowed to. This is a very important point, and one that we need to return to frequently; if we observe our thoughts just as the sky "observes" the phenomena passing before it, our minds will *gradually* become more spacious, reflecting clarity. But that's not what we usually do. Usually, we chase after thoughts with more thoughts, thinking them to be real.

Remembering this point is vital and takes time. In the book *The Joy of Living*, author Yongey Mingyur Rinpoche writes, "Just as space isn't defined by the objects that move through it, awareness isn't defined by the thoughts, emotions, and so on that it apprehends. Awareness like space, simply is."[10] Reflect on this metaphor for a moment: awareness, like space, simply is. Objects come into a particular space, either passing through it or occupying it briefly and temporarily, and then are gone. So too, our mind doesn't have to be defined by what arises within it; thoughts, ideas, impressions can all be allowed to pass through our mind without our grasping on to them. Another useful metaphor for the dynamics of thoughts arising within the mind is that of a train station. Trains pass through the station, yet the station is not the trains; it is a station for the trains. They arrive, stay a while, and then depart.

In the same way that clouds come and go, thoughts and emotions left to simply be, will arise, stay briefly, and then dissipate. It's only through focusing on and thinking about thoughts that they continue. Thinking about thoughts... hmm. So, our mind is not defined by the thoughts that pass through it. Practicing and realizing this, however, is easier said than done, but it is an important point to come back to whenever we find ourselves lost in the clouds of emotions and feelings. This is a potentially profound way of working with our mind and with the thoughts that arise in it—that we aren't our thoughts, that our "good" or "bad" thoughts have nothing to do with who we are. We'll come back to this again in the Chapter *Working with Our Thoughts*.

> For a moment, just relax, put this book down, and simply watch the stream of thoughts that arises within your mind. Don't try to alter the flow, don't try to control what arises. Simply and freely remain in the present with your thoughts. Allow your awareness to be like the space into which all manner of phenomena arise. Without judgment. Without thinking about your thoughts. That's all.

Returning briefly to the passengers in Terminal G, what was lacking in their various states of reactivity was the insight into how their emotions and feelings were exacerbating their stress rather than alleviating the problem. My guess is that some of these individuals, given their sheer numbers, suffered from varying health-related illnesses. I had to wonder what this stress, unchangeable in terms of the origin of the stressor, was doing to their bodies.

What happens to people when they "become patients" and are thrust into the odyssey of illness? What happens after the diagnosis, after the official proclamation, which can change the way that the person views her or himself in relation to the rest of the world? Oftentimes, the immediate tendency is to look to outer circumstances that can be controlled in order to change the outcome or trajectory of the given diagnosis.

Health-care practitioners are witnesses to the acute response of grief following the diagnosis of a life-threatening illness and the steady depletion of joy that follows the course of a chronic illness. We can easily empathize with and understand our patients' struggles with the emotional impacts of illness. But how do the acute and chronic stressors of our professional lives affect our wellness? What of the nurse who, after a full day at work, finds his patient lying on the floor in a puddle of urine, an abrasion on her knee. How can he cope with the thoughts that arise: *I was hoping to get out on time tonight! Damn, another incident report! If I didn't have such an unmanageable assignment, this never would have happened! Maybe I should have gone into law instead!*

What about the ER physician struggling with her mother's recent cancer diagnosis who enters the patient exam room to find a motherly woman in the final stages of her own battle with cancer? Flooded by the emotions and challenges of her personal life, she puts her own agenda—and feelings—on the back burner to attend professionally to the needs of her patient. Somewhere inside, however, the suffering of her own life becomes the seed of burden on her own intricate immune function and peace of mind.[11]

How can we handle our own suffering in a mindful and compassionate manner while also attending to the needs of another, acknowledging our own mind and its suffering while seeing our own suffering mirrored in the suffering of our patients? And, how do we attend to the immediacy of the present in their lives while maintaining the presence of our own mind?

What is required of us, if we are to be of utmost benefit to others, is nothing less than the transformation of our own mind. We need to look at who's showing up at the bedside and make sure that our presence of mind when we're attending to the needs of others is actually focused on the person in front of us. This requires of us a transformation of mind.

> Again, just relax, perhaps breathe a long out-breath, and simply watch the stream of thoughts that arises within your mind. Don't try to alter the flow; don't try to control what arises. Simply and freely remain in the present with your thoughts.
>
> Now, begin to notice what it is that your thoughts do? Do you think about your thoughts? Like waves in an ocean, can you just let them arise and then sink back into the mind, or do you begin to make up stories, imagine scenarios, create commentaries? Perhaps, when you begin to observe your thoughts without elaborating on them, they dissipate or become less substantial. Whatever happens, just let them float by, like clouds in the sky. Take some time, a few minutes, and just watch your thoughts, uninvolved.

The transformation of our mind begins when we start to take a look at its nature, its habits and patterns, from a nonjudgmental place. We must be able to *just be* with whatever thoughts are arising in our mind and whatever sensations are arising in our bodies without creating stories around them, without elaborating on them, and without the ongoing process of fabricating an anxious and ongoing stream of thought. Again, we need to review what our perceptions of ourselves are. Are we our thoughts? Our emotions? Are we our educational degree, designation, or profession? Or are we much more? (We are much more… and much less!)

As we review who we hold ourselves to be and who it is who minds the bedside, we may get glimpses into the impermanence of our thoughts, emotions, and sensations, seeing them more in their transient nature. Through an ongoing and committed practice to mindful, meditative, spacious awareness, we may find that we become more motivated to change how we relate to these brief phenomena of ourselves. We may even find ourselves impatient with the "old self," wanting to show up more fully at the bedside and in our lives.

Changing the way that we relate to our thoughts, feelings, emotions, and sensations takes time, and we need to be patient and compassionate with ourselves in the process. Because most of us have related to our phenomenal world and our perceptions about the world for the duration of our lives in a less-than-beneficial manner and because we have repeatedly reinforced our way of thinking, changing these patterns of heart and mind takes time. But we can make it enjoyable; it doesn't need to be a serious matter. Because the process of unfurling the banner of our truer nature is a lifelong process, let's have fun with it.

> Again, just relax, perhaps breath a long out-breath, and simply watch the stream of thoughts that arises within your mind. Don't try to alter the flow, don't try to control what arises. Simply and freely remain in the present with your thoughts.

> Whenever the mind attaches itself onto thoughts or distractions, simply bring it back to the breath. And then, once again, simply watch the flow of thoughts.

> Now, try to make a pleasant thought arise, one which is related to a situation or event that causes you to experience joy. Perhaps remember a time of play or leisure, a time when you were very happy doing something. It might be a memory of a beach or the mountains, perhaps a memory of time with

family or an event like a wedding or performance. Try to just stick with the thought and with the pleasant emotions that arise along with it. Try to remain in that state of mind. If you become distracted, bring your mind back to the thought. See if it's possible to stay with one pleasant thought as a singular phenomenon or whether the thought takes on a life of its own, evolving into stories, daydreams, memories. Try to go back to the pleasant thought, again and again.

No matter what happens, it's fine. Try it for five minutes, and then drop all thoughts, and relax.

In the previous exercise, what happened when you attempted to focus on one thought? Did your mind easily rest on the thought? Did it get distracted and start to think of other thoughts? Did you make up stories about that thought and create more thoughts? Did you perpetuate or lose the thought? Were you even able to focus on one pleasant thought as being more important than others, or did your mind take over and lead you into countless stories or other thoughts? Or perhaps, all thought disappeared? Whatever happened, it's fine. This is simply another way of becoming familiar with your mind.

It's a bit laughable, but when we start working with thoughts we may begin to see how fickle the mind is. Whether we have a good thought or a bad one, our thoughts require our attention to persist, and if we bring our mind back to the present moment, even the most persistent of thoughts can be released from our grasping at them. Keep this in mind.

Part of the universality of mindfulness, meditative awareness, and compassionate presence is that these practices are not limited by any particular philosophy or religion. While contemplative practices are the foundation of certain spiritual traditions, the dynamics of working with the mind are the same for all of us regardless of our religious, spiritual, or atheistic leanings. No matter what our background, our education, or our political inclinations are, our minds and the nature of our minds are the same:

- We're either distracted at any moment or we're not.
- We're either unconditionally compassionate toward another human being or we're not.
- We're either able to see another person's humanity humanely and without judgment or we're not.
- We're either in accord with our truest nature or we're not.

- We've either altered our present state of awareness with thoughts of the past and future—good and bad, want and aversion—or we haven't.

What prevents us from experiencing this unaltered mind, showing up at the bedside and experiencing another's "suchness," is our tendency to get stuck in stories about what is going on in our mind, rather than what is actually going on. We make up stories about our thoughts all of the time, thinking that this is who we are. We make a good decision about the care of a patient, who then recovers, and we're a "great nurse." We miss a detail in a treatment plan or overlook a new order, our patient declines (or dies!), and we're a bad nurse. We get recognized for our outstanding participation in committees and working groups, and we're "exceptional," or we can't take the stress of the hospital environment, and we're a "quitter." The list of labels and names is endless, and it's not limited to nurses; it's endemic to being human. We have so many labels for ourselves, all of which miss the mark in terms of addressing our truly compassionate and mindful self.

> What happens to our mind when we sit with the simple thought that who we are, here and now, right now, is good enough. What we've done up to this point in our life is enough. And whatever contributions we can make in the future toward bettering ourselves and the lives of others are bonuses. Where does our mind go when we allow it to relax into the state of feeling "okay" right here and right now? Where do our thoughts go? Just watch your mind as you triage your thoughts.

Combined with meditative awareness, when we give some space to our thoughts and emotions, we engage *a way of being* that allows us to have a sense of humor and appreciation for the way that we are, right here, right now.

> Where is your mind right now? What are you thinking? In which direction did it go?

The gradual realization of one's mind through mindfulness and meditative awareness is the development of a state of cognizance and compassion, where the division of self and other—good and bad, hope and fear—is dissolved into a clearer way of perceiving things, sometimes known as the purity of perception. While the realization of this "ultimate" way of being, consistently dwelling within such an uncontrived state, may seem unattainable at present, it is the *process toward* this way of being that brings clarity and compassion into our daily lives. The importance is our *motivation* to move in the direction of this state of nondistraction and realization, even if we don't realize it completely. In this way, minding the bedside, or minding our life, is not a goal; it is a way of being that can begin immediately, right now, at this moment, with each one of these words.

> As you are reading, your mind is conscious, to a certain degree, of the fact that you are reading. What else is your mind also aware of? The temperature of the room? Background noise? Any sensations in your body? How about things that you have to do as soon as you're done with this reading? Thoughts about whether this book is going to be what you expected it to be?

Without us "thinking about it," we have so many thoughts occurring from moment to moment! We show up at our patients' bedsides prepared to serve, only to find that we've lost our mind, or more appropriately, lost our mindfulness. With practice, as we become more mindful, we bring our mind back as soon as we realize that we're distracted and continue to attend to our patients. The nice thing is that since distraction is the norm, when we catch ourselves and return to the present, most likely, our patients will only notice a brief departure, if at all. What I've experienced frequently is that as long as I return to the bedside compassionately and attentively, my patients are grateful for me being there and care less about my temporary vacations.

In the book *Zen and the Brain*, author James Austin writes:

> Meditators discover a surprising fact when they finally arrive at moments of "no-thought": they do not have to think to be conscious. For consciousness starts with being aware. The awareness has a receptive flavor, its normal landscape is not a level plateau. Instead, it rises and falls as a series of peaks and valleys.[12]

As we work with our mind and begin to develop insight into its dynamics, we'll come to realize—even if slightly— that if we learn to follow after our thoughts less, returning repeatedly to the present moment, we'll find a quieter and more stable nature of our mind. Like the peaks and valleys that James Austin describes in his book, our thoughts and the topography of our mind is constantly changing. Our challenge comes from the habitual patterns of fearing the downhills and struggling with the uphills.

There is a simple but profound Tibetan expression that, *"Just as water if not stirred will become clear, mind too, if left unaltered, will find its true na-*

ture." Think about it. If we stir up a jar of water that has sand in it, it becomes cloudy and never becomes clear. In the same way, our mind is full of thoughts, similar to the sand, and if we're constantly stirring up our thoughts and emotions with more thoughts and more emotions, we will rarely glimpse a mind that is settled.

The profundity of this simple line lies *in the experience of realizing* that we are constantly altering our minds with our thoughts and feelings and with the elaboration on the thoughts that arise within it. Profoundly alarming is the fact that *we are so unaccustomed to not altering our mind with thoughts* that this simple advice can take years, if not a lifetime, to put into practice. It may be easy to imagine letting a vessel of water just sit, not stirring it with our hand. But how about our mind? Can we simply let it be, allowing it to settle into a state of nondistraction and equilibrium. Try it.

> Once again, allow your attention to rest on the flow of thoughts without elaborating any of them, without altering them. Watch the thoughts as they arise and *without creating stories around them,* allow them to fade into nonexistence. For a few minutes, or even moments, simply be...
>
> This time, if you become distracted during this short exercise, focus on the following line:
>
> ## SIMPLY WATCH YOUR THOUGHTS ARISE
> ## WITHOUT FOLLOWING THEM
>
> Try to remember the phrase, *"Just as water if not stirred will become clear, mind too, if left unaltered, will find its true nature."*

Was this difficult? What was the tendency of the mind? Perhaps you focused more on certain thoughts, elaborating ones that seemed more pertinent or important. Perhaps focusing on your thoughts actually resulted in brief periods where the flow of thought seemed to slow down. What is the nature of your mind when you're thinking? Did you find that the act of focusing on your thoughts could be interrupted by the flow of thought? Where did your mind go, and how quickly were you able to recognize your distraction and return to the task of observing your thoughts?

As we begin to work with our minds, we may find that so much of the time, our lives are based upon building thought upon thought, creating stories and themes around the thoughts, feelings, and emotions that arise. Rarely, if

31

ever, do we allow our thoughts to be "liberated" back into the realm from whence they came. As soon as a thought arises, we relate to it by either grasping onto it and creating more thoughts about it—a kind of *Alice in Wonderland* mindstream—or we dislike what we're thinking and say, "That's not me," and block such thoughts from arising...for the moment, anyway.

The *gift* of working with patients is that we can use our work with others as an invitation to mindfulness. When we begin to use interactions with those we serve as reminders to bring our mind home, we will automatically start showing up at the bedside more fully, being present with those we care for. The *gift* of working with our mind is that every moment—regardless of the time, of our mental state, of the circumstances—each and every precious moment is an invitation to awaken to a mind that is free from anxiety, from worries, from...itself.

Now, time for a timeout, time to take a break from whatever we're doing and have some playtime with our mind, time to watch our thoughts! We'll begin, as we did in the last chapter's exercise, by watching our breath, using it as the anchor of our attention. Now, please refer to Track #2, "Beginning With Your Thoughts." If you can, take some time with this exercise, allowing yourself to become familiar with it to the point that you can do it at any time, in any place, for any amount of time.

> Sitting on a straight-backed chair or couch or on a cushion on the floor, allow your body to become still. The back is straight without being stiff; the posture is relaxed, awake, and dignified. The hands can rest gently on the knees or in the lap. Settling into this moment, begin watching the breath.

> Become aware of the fact that you're breathing. Become aware of the movement of the breath as it flows into and out of the body. Feel the breath as it comes into the body and as it leaves the body. Simply remain aware of the breath flowing in and flowing out, not manipulating the breathing in any way. Simply being aware of it and noticing how it feels.

> Allow yourself to be with this flow of breath, coming in and going out. Notice the feeling of the breath as the lungs fill with air on the in-breath and deflate as you breathe out, the chest expanding and col-

lapsing. Perhaps feeling the breath in the abdomen, rising as you breathe in and flattening and sinking as you breathe out. Allow your attention to gently ride on the sensation of each breath, not thinking about breathing, without the need to comment. Simply watching your breathing.

As before, you'll probably notice that your mind wanders off to thoughts of the past, fantasies, memories, or regrets. Or it may move to anticipation of the future, planning, wishing, and judging. You may find yourself thinking about what you'll do after this exercise, what you have to do at work, things that you have to do.

This time, become aware of thoughts passing through the mind, noticing them but not engaging with them, allowing thoughts to be like clouds, drifting through a vast, spacious sky. If you find yourself carried away by a stream of thoughts or you notice that you are no longer observing right here, right now, in this moment, return to the breath, anchor yourself in the awareness of the breath, coming now to this breath. When you feel steady in the present, you can return again to witnessing the thoughts in the mind, allowing whatever is there to be there. Thoughts of fantasies, desires, likes, dislikes, memories, judgments, pressures of obligations. Aware perhaps of feelings or emotions: sadness, fear, joy, peace. Allowing all of your thoughts to simply emerge, as they are. Witnessing. Observing. Thoughts coming. Thoughts going. Not being drawn into analysis of those thoughts. Not pursuing them. Not rejecting or engaging the thoughts but seeing them as clouds in the vast, still sky of the mind.

Don't think about thinking. Watch the thoughts as an old man watches children at play—observing without being involved.

And now, drop all methods. Drop all thoughts. Just...relax.

For now, just work with noticing your mind and its thoughts. Don't try to do anything with your thoughts; neither cultivate them nor block them. Don't hang onto your good thoughts or try to push away your bad thoughts. Just be with them. The reason that we work with the breath first is to gain some stability in our mindfulness and our meditative awareness. As we begin to work with our thoughts, we may notice that our mindfulness is less stable. Part of the reason for this is that we actually believe that we are our thoughts; we believe that what we think is who we are. And as we begin to see the volume of thoughts that can arise and their impermanent and fleeting nature, we begin to see that maybe we were wrong. Maybe we really are more than our thoughts and our feelings.

As you begin to work with your thoughts, you may find that they seem to increase. You may become discouraged to find that where there was once only a slight buzz, there's now a loud rumble. It's okay. Because we have not spent a lot of time simply resting in our awareness of thoughts without elaborating on them or creating new stories about them, when we first begin to work with the mind and with the phenomena of thoughts, it may seem as if things get worse! Far from anything being wrong, this can be a good sign.

In his book *Coming to Our Senses*, Jon Kabat-Zinn writes:

> [W]hen you go deeply into stillness, it is amazing—all there is, is hearing yourself think, and it can be louder and more disturbing and distracting than any external noise…We may be shocked at what we discover, at how much of our thinking is chaotic and yet at the same time severely narrow and repetitive, shaped by much of our history and habits…When unattended, our thinking runs our lives without our even knowing it. Attended with mindful awareness, we have a chance not only to know ourselves better, and see what is on our minds, but also to hold our thoughts differently, so they no longer rule our lives.[13]

And, again from Sogyal Rinpoche's book:

> When people begin to meditate, they often say that their thoughts are running riot and have become wilder than ever before. But I reassure them that this is a good sign. Far from meaning that your thoughts have become wilder, it shows that you have become quieter, and you are finally aware of just how noisy your thoughts have always been.[14]

I put these quotes here as gentle reminders that the process of working with thoughts and becoming familiar with our mind is not simple. However, the challenges that we encounter as we do this are not unique to our mind or insurmountable; many, many thousands of people have learned to become more mindful, more aware, and more spacious with their minds and more compassionate with their hearts. It just takes time to get used to what, up until now, may have been out of our conscious awareness.

Again, read the following lines and then put the book down and practice being with your mind.

> As you become aware of your thoughts, what thoughts arise in response to them? Do you tend to block them out? Do you like to make up stories or elaborate on them? Are there thoughts that feel more pleasant than others? Is there a rescuer who jumps in to rescue you from the more difficult thoughts and feelings, perhaps a self who reminds you of your positive qualities and qualifications? Just watch this, as an old man would watch children at play. As you continue to watch your thoughts, do they sometimes disappear? Do you get a feeling of being detached from your thoughts, like you're watching a movie? Whatever the experience, just stay with it for a few minutes. And then just drop the watching and the experience, and relax in a state of calm abiding.

Summary and Reminders:

1.   Unable to control the thoughts and emotions that arise in our minds, we look for someone or something "out there" to blame for the way that we're feeling.

2.   Just as we can change our relationship with the weather by accepting that the clouds and storms are simply part of the landscape, we can intimately change our relationship with the "cloudiness" of our mind in how we relate to and perceive what arises.

3.   Grounding another's emotional distress through the heart of our own self-cherishing, realizing that our reactions to another's emotions have very little to do with "us," we can redefine who "we" are.

4.   We identify so strongly with our thoughts and emotions and with the stories that we make up in our minds that we not only believe them to be the truth but end up becoming them!

5.   In the same way that space isn't defined by what passes through it, nor is the sky defined by the clouds; so too, who we are has little to do with the arisings that occur in our mind.

6.   The transformation of our mind begins when we start to take a look at its nature, its habits and patterns, from a nonjudgmental place. It starts when we are able to *just be* with whatever thoughts are arising in our mind, whatever sensations are arising in our bodies, without creating stories around them or elaborating on them and without the ongoing process of fabricating impedimentary streams of thought.

7.   An essential quality of a mindful presence at the bedside is spaciousness—*spacious* in how we view our thoughts and, as best as possible, in each and every situation that we encounter.

8.   "Just as water if not stirred will become clear, mind too, if left unaltered, will find its true nature."

9.   The gift of working with our mind is that every moment—regardless of the time, of our mental state, of the circumstances—each and every precious moment is an invitation to awaken to a mind that is free from anxiety, from worries, from...itself.

10. Many times a day, check in with your mind. Bring it back again and again. As often as you remember, do this. You may even set a timer, your watch, a smart phone, something to help you to remember. Or put a very small reminder or sign up at work, maybe even something that is personal to you that will remind you to remind yourself.

11. As we begin to work with our minds, we may find that so much of the time, our lives are based upon building thought upon thought, creating stories and themes around the thoughts, feelings, and emotions that arise.

12. For now, just work with noticing your mind and its thoughts. Don't try to do anything with your thoughts; neither cultivate them nor block them. Don't hang onto your good thoughts or try to push away your bad thoughts. Just be with them.

13. Refer to Appendix B for a schedule on working the exercises from this chapter into your day.

Chapter 4

Compassion

Our feelings of impatience and frustration with ourselves in meditation are certainly understandable, especially when they persist in spite of our best efforts to overcome them. But as we sit in meditation we can begin to recognize the subtle violence inherent in our impatience with ourselves. As our awareness and understanding of our limitations in meditation continue to deepen, we begin to gain greater insight into what is happening. We realize we are catching ourselves in the act of perpetuating violence towards our wandering mind, our wayward will, or our sleepiness—in short, toward those very aspects of our self that need to be loved the most. We realize that to stop meditating simply because we feel we are not good at it amounts to abandoning the very aspects of our self that need patience and loving encouragement. We see that the whole venture in meditation is going to be a rough ride unless we can learn not to invade and abandon ourselves in response to all the ways in which meditation exposes our limitations and shortcomings. It is precisely at this point that we begin to appreciate the liberating power of compassion.[15]

—James Finley, author of *Christian Meditation:*
Experiencing the Presence of God

Having begun to work with our mind and its dynamics, we've gained some understanding of why our compassion may lag at times. Apart from the work-related stressors of assignments, dealing with chronically ill people, and the like, we also have a mind that has been habitually used to being lost in thoughts and stories. To bring our mind home and invigorate it with a compassionate presence and meditative awareness, we need to infuse our "real-life" practice with the components of mindfulness to watch our mind, awareness to remain present, and spaciousness to return again and again—with a sense of humor and perspective—to the mind. We need to know when we're distracted and to apply an antidote to our tendencies to judge what we find our mind doing. We need to find ourselves, to find our undistracted nature, within our minds, within our meditation. And, then...we need to have the "liberating power of compassion," as Finley so aptly puts it, to deal with the challenges that may arise when we're trying to put it all together.

The meditation and mindfulness that we're aiming our minds toward and that we want to cultivate as health-care professionals has to be based on the single goal of *alleviating others' suffering through changing the way that our mind works, becoming mindfully aware ourselves.* And, to do so, we must learn to be compassionate first with ourselves. As James Finley writes, "The whole venture in meditation is going to be a rough ride unless we can learn not to invade and abandon ourselves in response to all the ways in which meditation exposes our limitations and shortcomings." Finley's quote beautifully describes the compassionately spacious quality that we need to have with ourselves in order to learn how to mindfully attend to ourselves as well as others.

As health-care professionals, as caregivers, our reasons for helping another may vary, from the means of providing a paycheck for our family to a deep inner belief that our mission in life is to serve the sick. Helping is not always due to compassion but may be due to pity for the ill person, an ego-based drive for meaning in life, or—due to our professional inclinations—because it's our job.

The compassion that comes with a deep mindful presence is based on the realization that the person in front of me is no other than another me, another human who wishes to have happiness and to avoid suffering. Conceptually, compassionate mindfulness is a focused and attentive desire or intention to help another person due to a compassionate impulse based upon the realization that our patients suffer due to the very same mind "dynamics" that we encounter as we begin to practice mindfully aware. Profoundly, the only difference between my patients and me is that they're there and I'm here. In fact, at some point in our lives, many of us end up there and find out what it's like to be there!

As we develop a degree of stability within our mind, the compassion that emanates from our intentions will be less cluttered with distractions and judgments. As we become more aware, we become free of the clutter and are able to mindfully attend to another with compassion as the primary motivation for helping another. The rest of the details—job, paycheck, meaning—are the added benefits; the true value of learning to become compassionately mindful is that we become more whole, more true to who we really are as caregivers and as human beings.

In the health-care profession, isn't it usually the case that those who mentor us best are not just those with a theoretical basis of knowledge? We derive the greatest benefit from those who have integrated and who embody the knowledge that they're professing, those who have been at the bedside and have learned the practice of their art versus simple theory. In the same way, before we can even hope to develop genuine compassion for others, it is absolutely necessary for us to do so for ourselves. Although we may find that there are times when we attend to another with a genuine and unconditional compassion, the ability to attend first to ourselves compassionately, integrating and embodying this character, will be vital as we learn to be more mindful at the bedside. If we find ourselves exposed in our lack of mindfulness at the bedside, the compassion that we have for ourselves will bring our undivided presence back to the room.

The idea of compassion or even love for ourselves can cause us to squirm with discomfort. The idea that we need to love ourselves first can be seen as self-centered or selfish. Nothing is further from the truth. Remember patients who you've worked with who you would've done anything for. Remember how hard you worked, how much of yourself you put into their care. Don't you deserve that much respect? Don't you deserve that much care? Where have we gone wrong where we've equated selfishness at the expense of others for a genuine love for ourselves, compassion for ourselves? Why do we believe that caring for ourselves is any less important than caring for our patients?

Jesus said, "Thou shalt love thy neighbor as thyself."

The historical Buddha was quoted as saying, "You can search throughout the entire universe for someone who is more deserving of your love and affection than you are yourself, and that person is not to be found anywhere."

What is it about us that lacks this ability to love ourselves as we would our patients? To learn to become compassionate, we need to remember often what Finley wrote about needing to "realize we are catching ourselves in the act of perpetuating violence towards our wandering mind, our wayward will, or our sleepiness—in short, toward those very aspects of our self that need to be loved the most."

Although it is not always evident in our world, where we might wonder if love and compassion exist in an interdenominational and global context, most religious or spiritual tenets are based on a compassion that is thought to be an inherently human quality. In addition to its faith- or spiritually-based foundations, the qualities of an open heart are described in poetry, song, and story.

Working within a secular mind, not constrained by belief or spiritual practice, is something that any person can do, because we all have our minds and suffer to varying degrees from our mind's misapprehensions and misperceptions. Because the essence of compassionate caring is often found in the basic writings of spiritual traditions, and because learning another's basis for their beliefs is helpful to anyone working in health care, I'll provide here a few quotes and tidbits about compassion from sources related to Christianity, Judaism, Islam, Hinduism, and Buddhism. This group of quotes is far from exhaustive in its depth and is only meant to provide you with a glimpse of ideas from different spiritual traditions as they relate to compassion.

You may find that it is helpful to use one or more of the following quotes as an object of focus or contemplation when you're meditating on compassion. The words may evoke a sense within your mind that will help prevent you from straying into discursive thought.

In Christianity, the term *agape* is used to describe a selfless love or compassion felt for all people. From G. B. Caird's *Saint Luke*:

> The Greek language has three words for love, which enable us to distinguish Christian love (agape) from passionate devotion (eros) and warm affection (philia). Jesus did not tell his disciples to fall in love with their enemies or to feel for them as they felt for their families and friends. Agape is a gracious, determined, and active interest in the true welfare of others, which is not deterred even by hatred, cursing, and abuse, not limited by calculation of deserts or results, based solely on the nature of God. Love does not retaliate (vv. 27–31), seeks no reward (vv. 32–36), is not censorious (vv. 37–38). (p. 103)

William Barclay writes on agape, noting that:

> Agape has to do with the mind: it is not simply an emotion which rises unbidden in our hearts; it is a principle by which we deliberately live." (New Testament Words, 1977, p. 21.)

Gracious, determined and active interest aptly describes the kind of compassion that we're discussing in this chapter, a compassion that we achieve through working with and training our mind. Agape is one name for the kind of concern of the mind that doesn't seek its own self-interest, but the interest of others. Another name for this kind of concern is what is known in Judaism as *chesed*. It is one of the main virtues worth pursuing in life. In the book *Jewish*

Renewal, Michael Lerner writes:

> From the Jewish standpoint, chesed means loving-kindness, understanding others' complexities, recognition of inner and outer obstacles we all face in giving and receiving love, recognition and care.[16]

In the section of the book titled "God Intoxication," Lerner writes:

> Look for people who are constantly, almost unconsciously, engaged in little acts of caring and compassion for others, and who radiate a warmth and loving energy that is personal and specific (not the glazed eyes of "true believers" who tell you that they love you, but don't seem to notice who you are), the very focused love that comes from caring enough to get to know you in all your particularity, respects you for who you are and not just who they think you could or should be, and loves the God within you not as a separate part of your soul which needs to be liberated from the rest, but as a feature that flows through every part of your being.[17]

In *The Concept of Compassion in Islam* by Asghar Ali, written in the *Milli Gazette* (May 19, 2003), Mr. Ali writes that:

> In Islam, the Qur'an uses the word rahm (mercy, compassion) repeatedly. This word and its various derivatives have been used more than 326 times. According to Mufradat al-Qur'an by Imam Raghib, an authentic dictionary of the Qur'anic terms, rahmah means softening of the heart towards one who deserves our mercy and induces us to do good to him/her. It is interesting to note that the womb of a mother is also called rahm. Mother is always very soft towards her children (raqiq) and showers love and affection on them. Thus anyone who does so to others qualifies for rahm. Thus to cultivate rahm is to be faithful to one's mother.

In *The Ethics of Healing: The Oath of a Muslim Physician*, from the Qur'an, the prayer asks of God:

> Give us the wisdom to comfort and counsel all towards peace and harmony. Give us the understanding that ours is a sacred profession that deals with your most precious gifts of life and intellect. Therefore, make us worthy of this favored station with honor, dignity and piety so that we may devote our lives in serving mankind, poor or rich, literate or illiterate, Muslim or non-Muslim, black or white, with patience and tolerance,

43

with virtue and reverence, with knowledge and vigilance, with
Thy love in our hearts and compassion for Thy servants, Thy
most precious creation. (Qur'an, V/35)

One of the world's most ancient spiritual traditions, Hinduism, emphasizes the importance of compassion as follows:

Among the wealthy, compassionate men claim the richest
wealth,
For material wealth is possessed by even contemptible men.
Find and follow the good path and be ruled by compassion.
For if the various ways are examined, compassion will prove
the means to liberation
(Tirukkural 25: 241–242)

While each tradition emphasizes compassion as a practice for connecting
to God or the divine, as well as for connecting with one's fellow humans, the
various schools of Buddhism have expanded on what Sakyamuni Buddha (the
historical Buddha) taught about compassion, endeavoring—through hundreds
of discourses and teachings—to remind us that compassion is the element of
the mind that will help not only us, but all, to reach enlightenment. In the varied expressions of Buddhism, there are extensive practices, mantras (chants),
visualizations, and recitations designed specifically to invoke within the individual a deep sense of compassion for oneself and for all other beings.

In the book *Ethics for the New Millennium,* His Holiness the Dalai Lama
writes:

At a basic level, compassion (*nying je*) is understood mainly
in terms of empathy—our ability to enter into and, to some
extent, share others' suffering. But Buddhists—and perhaps
others—believe that this can be developed to such a degree
that not only does our compassion arise without any effort, but
it is unconditional, undifferentiated, and universal in scope. A
feeling of intimacy toward all other sentient beings, including
of course those who would harm us, is generated, which is
likened in the literature to the love a mother has for her only
child.[18]

Poetically, describing a kind of compassion where we aspire to be
whatever is necessary to alleviate the suffering of others, the eighth-century
Indian Buddhist scholar, Shantideva wrote, in the text *The Bodhicharyvattara*
(verses 17–20):

May I become food and drink in the aeons of famine for those poverty-stricken suffers.

May I be a doctor, medicine and nurse for all sick beings in the world until everyone is cured.

May I become never-ending wish-fulfilling treasures materializing in front of each of them as all the enjoyments they need.

May I be a guide for those who do not have a guide, a leader for those who journey, a boat for those who want to cross over, and all sorts of ships, bridges, beautiful parks for those who desire them, and light for those who need light.

And may I become beds for those who need a rest, and a servant to all who need servants.

May I also become the basic conditions for all sentient beings, such as earth or even the sky, which is indestructible.

May I always be the living conditions for all sentient beings until all sentient beings are enlightened.

Transcending the spiritual aspects of compassion, Einstein understood the nature of compassion as it relates to unity. In a poetic glimpse of his understanding of the relatedness of all things, he wrote:

A human being is a part of the whole called by us "Universe," a part limited in time and space. He experiences himself, his thoughts, his feelings, as something separate from the rest—a kind of optical delusion of his consciousness. The delusion is a kind of prison for us, restricting us to our personal desires and to affection for a few persons nearest to us. Our task must be to free ourselves from this prison by widening our circle of compassion to embrace all living creatures and the whole of nature in its beauty. Nobody's able to achieve this completely, but striving for such achievement is in itself a part of the liberation and a foundation for inner security.[19]

And finally, from the book *Zen and the Brain,* in which the arts of science and meditation meet in an exquisite union, author James Austin writes:

True compassion means we correctly perceive a situation, sense how it would affect us, project our feelings sympathetically toward the other person, *and then reach out selflessly* to respond in the most sensitive, appropriate way. In this manner does fully ripened compassion, subtly informed by the most enlightened wisdom, deliver the milk of human kindness deftly, *non*intrusively.[20]

What each of these passages address are ways of being, ways of relating to others; they're ways of seeing beyond our limited mind, our limited vision. True compassion, derived from the religious and spiritual traditions, asks us to transcend ourselves. It asks us to loosen the veil between self and other and see another as self. And it asks us to put aside our discursive mind and just be present with those whom we serve.

As health-care practitioners, we are often asked to put aside our own needs, comforts, and preferences in deference to those of our patient or client. But there's a difference between doing so because it is our obligation or even because we are concerned about the clinical outcomes—and hence our professional reputations—and because we truly believe that our patient's welfare is as important, if not more so, than our own.

In reflecting on how we engage the act and presence of compassion, it may be striking for us to realize that amongst the many things that we have been taught in our careers, the many faces of compassion, actual practices in compassionate presence are notably lacking. In the book *Medicine and Compassion—A Tibetan Lama's Guidance for Caregivers*, coauthor Dr. David Shlim writes:

> It's ironic that this lack of overt compassion in medicine comes at a time when medicine can do more for a patient than at any time in history. Major advances of the past fifty years include antibiotics, anti-inflammatories, sophisticated non-invasive diagnostic capabilities, minimally invasive surgical techniques, immunization against a wide variety of diseases, kidney dialysis, open-heart surgery, and organ transplant. Despite these remarkable achievements, few people seem as happy as they should be with the way medicine is practiced. Surveys show that doctors are less satisfied with their careers than ever before, patients often complain about their medical care, and the people who manage healthcare systems throw up their hands at making medicine affordable or universally available. A piece of the puzzle is missing, and that missing piece may be compassion.[21]

This missing puzzle piece is part of the presence that we engage when we are practicing from the heart of an awakened mind, a mind in which mindfulness, awareness, and a spacious attitude reside. When we're minding the bedside, our compassion should be in how we are and in how we *become*, and in how our patients experience our presence when we're with them. True compassionate caring at the bedside breaks down the barriers of separation that we can erect in order to protect ourselves from the suffering that we encounter on a day-to-day basis. Seeing another as another self, an-other-me, or at least as another precious human—capable of experiencing happiness and suffering, joy and hope—is at the root of a compassionate mind.

Sometimes in health care we lose the ability to recognize that our patients are similar to us. When our only experience of another is through their suffering, when we only know them as "a diagnosis," or refer to them as the "patient," while it protects us from the pain that they may endure, it separates us from another self, same as we are, and reduces them to "the other." I clearly remember times, too many times, while working in the intensive-care setting, when I would refer to my patient as "the heart" in room number one or "the GI bleed" coming into room three. While subtle, this jargon of designating people as their illnesses removed me from their humanness and from their just-like-me-ness.

Now we're going to practice a basic method of arousing compassion, starting first with watching the breath and then evoking a feeling of love, allowing our mind to focus on the physiology of love. Please refer to Track #3, "Caring for a Loved One," which you can download from my website.

> Relax and begin by watching your breath. You'll use your breath as an anchor for your attention, and if you become distracted, bring your mind back to the breath. Just remain in this space, abiding calmly for a few minutes. When your mind becomes distracted, bring it back to the breath.

> Now, picture in your mind someone in your life who is or has been a source of deep love. It might be a parent, spouse or partner, or child. Just vividly picture someone who has been very loving to you or who you deeply love and who has taught you what it means to love and to be loved. Allow the feeling of this love to rise within your mind, and feel the physiology of this love in your body. Do this for a short while.

> Now, imagine that this person who has given you so much love, who you love so dearly, is the pa-

tient that you're caring for. Feel the added sense of urgency in needing to alleviate their suffering, and feel your own discomfort at seeing this loved one suffer so much. Get a sense of how your mind is and how your physiology changes when you compassionately imagine how much you want to alleviate this person's suffering. Be with these thoughts, feelings, and sensations for a brief moment.

Take note of any sensations in your body, emotions, or thoughts in your mind, and see if what arises is an association of love or whether other thoughts and emotions come into play.

How easy is it to give rise to a deep and abiding feeling of love for this person? Are you able to experience this same physiology when you're with your patients?

And then relax and let go of any sort of effort, simply remaining in this state of mind for a while.

The compassion that Finley states that we need for ourselves is the very same compassion that we need for others, realizing that the "meditation" of our patients is on their illness and that most patients are constantly "perpetuating violence…toward those very aspects of… [themselves]…that need to be loved the most." How often have we heard a patient, in sadness, cry out, "What did I do to deserve this?" The very same lack of compassion that we often feel toward ourselves is magnified in a person whose life and circumstances feel out of control. When we meet a person's pain with pity, they feel less than, diminished, pitiable. When we are able to meet another who is suffering with the recognition of compassion, that we all have within ourselves this root of suffering, we help to heal their self-flagellation…and ours too!

Mindful compassion emphasizes an aspiration as well as an awareness; while we may not be able to actualize it, to remain in an uninterrupted flow of selfless compassion, it will become our aspiration, our goal, to be in that state or to bring our mind back home to that state as much as is possible. And, within that state, our sole intention for remaining mindful is to help others as well as to help ourselves.

The kind of awareness that helps our patients heal is addressed poignantly in a passage in Robert Wicks's book *Overcoming Secondary Stress in Medical and Nursing Practice.* While not specifically about compassion, it beautifully illustrates how our own compassionate presence can have a positively "contagious" effect on our patients. This passage, excerpted from a chapter titled *The Simple Care of a Hopeful Heart*, describes an encounter that Doctor Wicks had when working with a patient who had made remarkable progress within the therapeutic relationship:

[Dr. Wicks:] "Let's stop for a moment. I have a couple of questions."

She was in the middle of a story, so she was a bit surprised but did as I asked and responded, "What are they?"

"Picture my eyes as a mirror. As you look at them, what do you see?"

She smiled radiantly, showing that she would enjoy this exercise, and said, "I see a person filled with great life. Someone who is excited that she is finally able to find the joyous little girl in herself who had been there before but was lost due to abuse. She has now combined that child with the full grown woman she is now." Then, after a pause, she added with a big smile, "*And*, she is thoroughly happy about it all!"

"Yes." I told her, "That's what I see, too. Given this, the second question I have for you is how did you get to this point? When you first came to see me, you weren't in this place."

My expectation was that she would provide a fairly detailed review of the concrete steps that she took to change her way of viewing herself and the world. Instead, she made a half frown, looked straight at me with her dark brown eyes, and said, "You mean you really don't know?"

Taken a bit off guard, I responded, "No. I really don't exactly know."

"Well, it was easy." She said.

> *When I first came to see you,*
> *I simply watched the way you sat with me.*
> *Then I began sitting with myself in the same way.*

For a while I was silent. I had forgotten how a respectful presence to others could be so transformative. Such a gentle way of being with others opens up possibilities that are not there when they are able to view themselves only in narrow, unnecessarily negative and distorted ways.[22]

The "respectful presence" that Wicks writes of reminds us that by helping ourselves to become more compassionately present, more respectful of our inherent nature, we can more fully benefit others. And this presence is based upon a motivation to be more present for the service to others. Each person with whom we engage when we're in an undistracted state stands to benefit from our presence because they can be seen for who they are, without the veils of our judgments and stereotypes. Even those whom we might not ordinarily think of—the grocery clerk, the movie ticket taker, the "jerk" on the road who absent-mindedly cut us off in traffic—can benefit from our being more present and compassionate. In fact, everyone stands to benefit because of the web of interdependence; the grocery clerk or bad driver who is dealt with compassionately may then go home and *not* kick the dog, yell at the kids, or have one too many drinks.

As we awaken to the compassionate nature of our mind and slowly dissolve the conceptual, judging mind—or at least as we learn to give it a rest and we become more adept at remaining in the moment-to-moment awareness—a compassionate response, a respectful presence, will begin to develop. As we become more other-centric and less self-centric, mindfulness will become a progressive process where we find more unity and less duality between another and ourselves. And through this unity, a kind of clarity of mind based on kindness and compassion will evolve. In the book *Medicine and Compassion—A Tibetan Lama's Guidance for Caregivers*, coauthor Chokyi Nyima Rinpoche writes:

> Deeply felt kindness and compassion generates a clarity of mind, a sense of being present for the persons you are caring for. When a doctor or nurse truly cares for a person, these feelings can produce a kind of attentiveness that makes it more difficult to make mistakes or errors in judgment. This kindness and concern also inspires confidence in the patient. The patient is able to relax, to be more at ease in a difficult situation. When the doctor has an honest and kind face and speaks words that show true concern and care, the sick person feels it a hundred times more than any other person would.[23]

A final point on compassion is that as we begin to become more forgiving with ourselves and are able to see our patients in their humane entirety, we'll also begin to develop perspective on our peers' needs and quirks. In my many years in nursing, it has always dismayed me that nurses can be so disparaging toward one another. I am aware of colleagues with whom I have worked who I knew were suffering through their own mental obstacles but with whom I simply could not connect. My own discursiveness of mind prevented me from relating to these people as "another me" in need of compassion. What I've gradually realized through my own practice is that if I can't show up for my peers as easily as for those I'm caring for, then I've probably got more work to do with my own forgiveness. A good bit of food for thought.

We're going to end this chapter with a short loving-kindness practice. In this practice, we take a tangible sense of love within our mind, within our ex-perience, and after establishing this we use this feeling and attitude and prac-tice directing it toward others. It's a great practice to get used to the immediacy of the bedside environment and to being able to engage this practice instan-taneously. What it does is to allow us to see that we always have within our mind the ability to arouse this sense of love and appreciation and to use this inherent trait of the mind within our nursing practice. Please download Track #4, " Loving-Kindness Practice" from my website.

> As we've done at other times, begin by finding an unhurried place and time or at least finding these qualities within your mind. Beginning with the breath, just settle into yourself, calming the mind, freeing it from distractions and preoccupations. Whatever else is going on in your life will wait for a few minutes while you do this exercise.

> After you've maintained a minimal level of distrac-tion within your mind, just as you did in the previ-ous exercise, picture in your mind someone in your life who is or has been a source of deep love. It might be a parent, spouse or partner, or child. Just vividly picture someone who has been very loving to you or who you deeply love and who has taught you what it means to love and to be loved. Allow the feeling of this love to rise within your mind, and feel the physiology of this love in your body.

> After you've established the feeling of love in your body, begin to imagine directing that same love toward the person who evoked this feeling within you. Imagine that this love is emanating from you

and going directly toward this person. If it enhances the feeling, you can imagine it streaming from your heart or the center of your chest, or you can see this person and imagine them receiving this feeling of love from you. Some people find that they can do this exercise more easily if they imagine or visualize a color or stream of light, or perhaps a mistlike stream emanating from themselves to the other person. Please do whatever works for you and whatever enhances your ability to concentrate and focus. Do this for a short while, coming back to the breath as an anchor whenever you find yourself distracted.

Next, picture in your mind a patient who you've cared for who evoked a sense of appreciation, affection, or even love. If you can't picture the person clearly, just get a "feel" for the individual, connect with a physical or emotional aspect of how you felt (or still feel if you're presently caring for them) when you cared for this person. Continue with this exercise for a while.

Now just as you did when you directed a feeling of love toward the person familiar to you, do the same with this person. Allow a feeling of immeasurable compassion for this person to arise and direct it from yourself, from your mind, to this person. Stay with this for a while, always remembering to come back to the breath when you find yourself distracted.

Imagine that this love or compassion is emanating from you and going directly toward this person. As before, if it enhances the feeling, you can imagine it streaming from your heart or the center of your chest, or you can see this person and imagine them receiving this feeling of love from you.

If you find that you have difficulties visualizing this process, just allow the feelings to arise in your mind, allow the intention to remain in your mind. Maintain the focus, remembering to come back to the breath when you find yourself distracted.

And now, relax. Just be. Drop all methods. Remain in the undistracted state of the mind, calmly abiding.

Summary and Reminders:

1. The meditation and mindfulness that we're aiming our minds toward and that we want to cultivate as health-care professionals has to be based on the single goal of *alleviating others' suffering through becoming mindful ourselves.*

2. The compassion that comes with a deep mindful presence is based on the realization that the person in front of me is no other than another me, another human who wishes to have happiness and to avoid suffering.

3. True compassionate caring at the bedside breaks down the barriers of separation that we can erect in order to protect ourselves from the suffering that we encounter on a day-to-day basis.

4. For us, when we're minding the bedside, the truest definition of compassion should be in its action and in its manifestation—*how* we arrive at our most compassionate nature and how our patients experience our presence when we're with them.

5. Please turn to Appendix C for the schedule on how to practice exercises during the day. This can include using a one-minute "tune-up" exercise that you can use anytime that you have a brief break at work. In a one-minute tune-up, you simply establish your awareness of the breath, watch the thoughts in your mind, direct feelings of warmth and compassion toward anyone who you think of, and relax. Additionally, go to my website for new downloads and practices.

Chapter 5

Working with Our Thoughts

All day I have been uncomfortably aware of the wrong that is in me. The useless burden of pride I condemn myself to carry, and all that comes with carrying it. I know I deceive myself as a monk and a writer, but I cannot catch myself in the act. I do not see exactly where the deception lies.[24]

—Thomas Merton, author of *A Vow of Conversation: Journals 1964–1965*

I was on call, doing hospice work in rural Maine. It was late in the day, and I'd just finished admitting a patient with whom I was not supposed to discuss dying, even though he was in a semicomatose state and was in fact dying. Even still, it had been a good visit; the patient was staying at a friend's home, blessed by a friendship that allowed him to die in a nurturing setting. When I'd first arrived, I'd been frustrated by a mindless gap in which I'd not caught an error in directions and had overshot my exit by 20 miles. I'd completely lost presence of mind and had become so frustrated that—at one point on the highway—I'd contemplated (not seriously, of course!) turning around and going home, just leaving the patient, friends, and family. Cancel the evaluation, admit my deficiency of mind, and go home to suffer this momentary lapse in reason…and probably get fired!

Fortunately, I'd been aware enough to notice that I'd lost my mind(fulness) and had the presence in the moment to complete the evaluation and admission in perfect form, glad that I'd had the opportunity to be of service and get someone who truly needed it into hospice care. I'd become aware of my frustration in time to bring my awareness to the moment, rest my mind in what I was doing, and give my momentary distraction enough space in which to dissipate.

The "problem" that night was that the burden of my mind and its frustrations were distracting me from the important nature of what I was doing and from a genuinely compassionate intention to help others in the end of their lives. The distractions were that I was on call; that I had another visit that I had to make; and that I was tired, uninspired, and wishing to be in the coziness of home and not driving through rural Maine. I had let myself get too focused on the missed exit and the factors that I couldn't control and had forgotten about the one thing that I had some control over: my mind!

I left my first appointment and begrudgingly set off to a visit that I believed, in all of my frustration, should have been done earlier by the primary nurse, not the on-call nurse. On the way to the call I was confronted with more challenges: fatigue, lack of street signs and streetlights, a blowing storm, and darkness. All of the external things that I could ever hope to blame were in the picture.

I finally arrived at my destination, a wicked wind blowing outside, and entered apologetically. It was the home of an elderly man who was supposed to begin on an intravenous morphine pump. Friends and relatives were gathered in the home—good people, guardians of the dying, the essential blessings that anyone can truly have in life. When I made my way into the bedroom, standing at the bedside was the wife of the dying man. Her husband was in bed, relatively unresponsive, eyes glazed, breathing rapidly. Looking at him, I suddenly remembered why I was there...not the pump! I began an assessment, and it was clear to me that he was not in need of morphine; he was in need of a guide, a midwife into death.

I sat next to him at the bedside and began talking quietly to him, reassuring him that he was safe and in the good hands of those whom he loved and who loved him. Within three minutes, his breathing slowed and his pulse thinned and began to disappear. I asked his wife to come take the seat that I had occupied...quickly. At that very moment, two daughters arrived from out of town. The wife cried out, "Girls, quick, come here!" And as they came through the door and came to the bed, their father, "my patient," peacefully died, with his family at the bedside, free of pain, and free of an intervention that would have proved unnecessary.

I share this story because it's one of transformation of the mind—my mind, to be more precise. The night had been difficult, my mind out of sorts, distracted, off-kilter. It was only through mindfully returning to the present, becoming aware that I'd become so fundamentally distracted, and getting to the needs of the present—the immediacy of the moment—that I'd recognized the patient's need to be shepherded into death. He needed my presence, not my assessment or my pump or anything other than a graceful and compassionate attention to who he was and where he was going. Had I not summoned a state of compassionate presence in that moment, based on comprehending what it was that he really needed, there is the likelihood that I would not have attended to him and would have missed the moment. I would have failed to attend to his death and would have started the pump, "relieving his pain." Instead, it was a moment of magic, one that I shared with the family and that we all discussed after the immediacy of his death had passed.

Our ability to change the quality of our lives and the lives of others depends to a great deal on our ability to be present with the world, with others, and with the circumstances—all of them—that life presents to us. Our ability to be present with the world depends upon our ability to be stable within our minds, moment to moment, consistently, with whatever is going on. Our ability to be present with our patients depends on our ability to be here now, to be present—now, while reading this line—without distractions, without following any other thoughts.

Whether working with our thoughts, feelings, sensations, or emotions, the methods are the same. The point of mindfulness and meditative awareness is to return repeatedly to the undistracted nature of our minds. We do this by leaving the sensory phenomena within the senses that they arise from; that is, we "leave the seeing in the seeing, leave the hearing in the hearing, leave the thinking in the thinking."[25] What this means is that when a thought arises, we leave it in the realm of thinking and return to the undistracted and unaltered nature of our minds. And when we hear something or see something that distracts us, we "leave" that phenomenon within the realm that it occurred. We allow the things that we see, the sounds that we hear, and the thoughts that we think to arise within their place of origination—the sense consciousness that perceived them—and return back to our undistracted mind. In this way, by treating each piece of information or input as a phenomenon of its sense "organ," we can remain less distracted by its presence.

Leaving things as they are *can be a lot harder than one might imagine.* We are so accustomed to following the thoughts and sensations that arise that we don't actually know how not to follow them. We see something that arouses a positive or negative thought, and we follow it. Or we hear something that we like, for example praise, or something that we don't like, for example blame, and we create more stories around what we hear. What's important is that we realize that this is happening, that we begin to familiarize ourselves with our tendencies, and that we start to become comfortable with the habits of our mind. The most important thing is that we integrate into our practice this idea of leaving things as they are, of not trying to eliminate whatever arises, but—

instead—of allowing them to simply be without creating stories around them.

What do I mean by "creating stories"? Creating stories—elaborating on thoughts and temporary arisings in our mind—is what we do when our attention drifts from the present to either the past or the future. We are used to using our mind this way: elaborating one thing upon another. An ache turns into a terminal illness, a thought turns into a past discussion, a criticism turns into an opportunity to flagellate ourselves for all of our misdeeds. One thought leads to another. The pity is that we do this when we're supposed to be attending to the needs of another. We're in seeing a patient or client, and something that they say or do stimulates a thought, idea, or memory from a similitude of thoughts that we bear around our own experiences. All of a sudden, it's no longer about the patient, it's about us…we're gone, lights on, but no one is at home.

In his book *Insight Meditation*, Joseph Goldstein describes this kind of checking-out when he writes:

> When we lose ourselves in thought, thought sweeps up our mind and carries it away, and in a very short time we can be carried far indeed. We hop a train of association not knowing that we have hopped on, and certainly not knowing the destination. Somewhere down the line we may wake up and realize that we have been thinking, that we have been taken for a ride. And when we step down from the train, it may be in a very different state of mind from where we jumped aboard.[26]

Our patients know it when we've checked out, when we've boarded a train of association and have left the station of present awareness. Inversely, they know and feel it when we're really there with them. Being "really there with them" depends on how well we can work with the thoughts and the distractions that create a constant stream within our minds. Mindfulness, meditative awareness, and attentiveness to the present all help us to remain mentally with our patients for the entirety of the time we're physically with them.

How we begin to work with nonattachment to the phenomena that arise in our minds is by realizing that everything is impermanent, even the apparently real thoughts and emotions that arise with our minds! Our attraction to a particularly good-looking person or our aversion to a particularly negative person are also impermanent and fade away. When we look at the world around us, especially when we look at those we care for, we see the constant dance, the dynamic flux of birth, life, and death. We realize through our daily interactions with those who are ill or dying that this life that we hold so dear will ultimately disappear. Our patients' lives are still impermanent—they're still going to die— even when our interventions cure. We are constantly reminded of the impermanence of it all. We won't get too deep into this right now because what we need to focus on is the impermanence of the phenomena that occur within our minds. Still, it's good to remember when we start taking our thoughts too seriously.

What we realize as we work more and more with mindfulness and attending to our minds is that all the phenomena that occur internally—everything that we experience within the perception of our mind and senses—is transitory, ephemeral. We have a thought, hear a noise, taste some food, have an encounter with our patient; and then, within a period of time, it's all gone. Therefore, our task in learning to dwell within the compassionate and mindful state of being is to continually remind ourselves that whatever pulls us from our anchor of mindfulness and compassion is temporary, however real it may appear.

To get to the immediacy of the mind and its present cognizant awareness, we work first with the breath as the anchor, as we have already done. The next thing that we do is become aware of the flow of our thoughts, which we touched on a bit in Chapter 3. What we may have noticed is that, just as each breath comes and goes, so does every thought and sensation. Our minds are constantly occupied with one thing or another. Our job is to not get caught up in anything in particular but to return to and remain in the simple awareness of the undistracted and unaltered nature of our mind. This is done by repeatedly and repeatedly returning to an object of focus—for example, this sentence— each and every time that we find ourselves distracted.

The challenge or opportunity is to remind ourselves that we are distracted, that our attention has drifted, and then to skillfully and compassionately bring our minds home again and again. To do this, to work with the transient arisings of thoughts, emotions, feelings, and sensations, we need to remain aware that we are being mindful, that we are in the moment, or even that we are distracted. While, as beginners, we constantly have to put a great effort into remaining mindful and aware, eventually—just as breathing is involuntary and inherent to our existence—it should be our aspiration to be able to effortlessly remain mindful and to return, whenever we become distracted, back to the nature of our pure awareness.

Again, returning to impermanence, it is through our meditative awareness and our awareness of our mindfulness that we realize that each thought, each arising idea or impulse, is transient and fleeting. Gradually, as we become more comfortable with the reality that all of the ideas that we hold so dear—

ideas about life, about ourselves, about our patients—are impermanent, we'll become less attached to the "self" that we tend to hold in rigid definition. We'll begin to see that this self is constantly changing based on our thoughts and experiences, and we may even come to connect with the self that is beyond these passing phenomena. With this more spacious self, we'll gradually begin to tear down the barrier between "self" and "other," and with this falling away of interpersonal duality, we'll find the wellspring of a compassion that doesn't create the distinction between "nurse" and "patient," "surgeon" and "case." Instead, we'll begin to see the other as another "me."

Let's take time now to do a brief exercise that will begin to give us an idea of how to work with and view *without attachment* the dynamic of the arising phenomena that occur with our mind. Up until this point, we've focused on using the breath as our anchor or we've taken time to watch the thoughts that occur in the mind. What we'll do now is to drop any particular focus and "simply remain" with whatever thoughts, ideas, and perceptions are occurring in the moment. To really remain undistracted with whatever arises is quite difficult, so we'll practice this with the idea of nonjudgment in mind, allowing whatever arises to simply be. As in previous chapters, you can read along with this script or you can refer to Track #5, "Working with Our Thoughts," available for download from my website.

> Just as we've begun our previous exercises, begin by sitting on a straight-backed chair or couch or on a cushion on the floor. Or, if you're taking a few moments during the day or time out of work, simply rest in whatever environment that you find yourself. Since we will eventually want to practice in any situation, ultimately it doesn't matter where we are as much as where our attention is. Allow your body to become still. The back is straight without being stiff; the posture is relaxed, awake, and dignified. The hands can rest gently on the knees or in the lap. Settling into this moment, begin watching the breath.
>
> Now, as in the previous exercise, become aware of the fact that you're breathing. Become aware of the movement of the breath as it flows into and out of the body. Feel the breath as it comes into the body and as it leaves the body. Simply remain aware of the breath flowing in and flowing out, not

manipulating the breathing in any way. Simply being aware of it and noticing how it feels.

Allow yourself to be with this flow of breath, coming in and going out. Notice the feeling of the breath as the lungs fill with air on the in-breath and deflate as you breathe out, the chest expanding and collapsing. Allow your attention to gently ride on the sensation of each breath, not thinking about breathing, without the need to comment. Simply watching your breathing.

Allow your attention to turn toward your mind and toward any thoughts that may arise. Simply watch your mind. When you become distracted, bring your mind back to the breath as an anchor, and then when you've refocused, return your attention to your thoughts.

Once you've watched your thoughts, "drop" the need to watch them and simply rest in the atmosphere that you've created without particularly trying to "do" anything. It's almost like floating on a raft in the water. You don't need to hold the raft up for it to float; you can simply be supported by the raft. In the same way, allow your attention to simply be supported by your mind watching its thoughts, without particularly doing anything.

What happens as you watch your thoughts? Just notice. Do they get stronger or weaker? Do they seem to fade away? Maybe you experience a kind of clarity without thoughts? Whatever happens is fine. Just be in the place of watching your mind, watching your thoughts, without following them.

Once you've tried this for a while, simply let go of everything and rest in the space that you've created for a while.

What did we find when working on remaining? We may have noticed that our minds tend toward trying to find a place to "hang our hat," that we are uncomfortable without having someplace to "place" our minds, that simply resting in an expansive space either spaces us out or leads us to sleep. Or, as is usually the case, we find that our minds simply wander off in multiple directions without really attending to the present pure awareness. Whatever happens, it is exactly as it should be. Even recognizing for a moment that we've become distracted is a step toward the liberation from our otherwise restless mind that spends less time "at home" than we'd ever imagined.

I remember the first time that I bumped into what I would almost call a confusion that arose when I didn't try to find a place to place my mind, when resting my mind "in the mind" wasn't associated with a place. There was an immediate disconnect, a longing for a "home" for my attention. I'd always grounded my attention in following thoughts and making up thoughts about the thoughts, thinking about the thinker. The experience of just having the awareness of bare attention was so disconcerting because I had always associated my mind with the activity of thinking versus just being. In Buddhism, there's a concept described as *thoughts without a thinker*. What this means is that through the process of becoming more aware, we can gain some distance from the phenomena that arise within the mind and look at them without "ownership," without trying to place our mind into the realm of our thoughts. In many traditions, this kind of unaltered or uncluttered mind refers to a cognizant or knowing quality that doesn't have to be involved with the constant chatter that we often associate with our mind. This may sound abstract at present, but as we return to it more and become more adept at working with the mind just resting within itself, we'll open to a more experiential quality of what this means. We'll begin to get hints of a "mind" that can simply recognize, cognize, and observe without being any "where."

Because we're so unfamiliar with just allowing our minds to "be" in the present, we spend our lives making up stories about who we are and attempting to locate ourselves in some category—"I'm a nurse, a bike rider, a father, a husband, a writer, a...whatever!" And, to a certain extent, in how I negotiate my way in this world, this is who I am. But when it comes to my mind, is my mind any one of these attributes? Is my mind singular or multiple? That is, is each thought part of the mind or an expression of it? And if the thoughts are simply the phenomena of the mind, then how real are they? If my mind were only the constant stream of thoughts, sometimes coherent and other times disjointed, then it would be a strange organism indeed, and I would be going in millions of directions at once, which I sometimes do when my mind isn't focused. In fact, if "my mind" were actually made up of its thoughts and patterns, it would constantly flicker in and out of being—morphing, changing in its dynamics and in its directions. It would probably look more like a subatomic particle!!

So why all this focus on thoughts? By now it may seem obvious that our minds, and by extension our thoughts, cause us much of our suffering both at the bedside and in our lives. When our minds are distracted, we lose the quality of attention that is necessary to serve our patients in our fullest and most compassionate capacity. And when our minds are negative or filled with discursive thoughts about who we are, we lose the capacity to simply be, whether at the bedside or the dinner table.

Thoughts are not the problem! No, they really aren't. Just as the sun's rays are the natural emanation of the sun, our thoughts are the expression of our mind. But we wouldn't say that the sun's rays are the sun. They are an aspect of the sun, a phenomenal representation of its brilliance and radiance. In the same way, our thoughts are the natural radiance of our mind. Or, in working with the metaphor of an ocean, thoughts are like the waves in the ocean, arising and then settling. Our mind is the ocean from which springs all manner of thinking: happy thinking and sad thinking, benevolent thinking and nasty thinking, creative thinking and stagnant thinking. So why do we assume that our thoughts are our minds? If we can allow the thoughts to simply come and go, much as we've done in our exercises, then we can begin to establish a different relationship with them. Instead of being swayed and buffeted by their arising, we can look at them as the phenomena of the mind, neither good nor bad. Eventually, we'll be able to view even the most difficult thoughts and emotions with a sense of distance and space and won't cling so tightly to the notion that "they" are "me."

Now, let's take the previous exercise and distill it down to a few phrases.

Allow your body to become still.

Become aware of the movement of the breath as it flows into and out of the body.

Simply watch your breathing.

Allow your attention to turn toward your mind and toward any thoughts that may be arising.

Don't try to do anything with your thoughts; just watch without chasing after past thoughts, anticipating future thoughts, or prolonging present thoughts.

When you become distracted, bring your mind back

to the breath as an anchor, and then when you've refocused, return your attention to your thoughts.

Simply watch your mind.

In order to begin to gain some stability within our mind, we need to do this exercise many, many times a day. By getting into the habit of momentarily bringing mindfulness and awareness to the mind in order to observe it, using the breath as an anchor for the attention, we can begin to gain an awareness of how our mind normally works. By repeatedly working with our mind, gradually we'll find that the thoughts that used to pull us away from the present have less force.

> Just a reminder and tip for working with the mind. Try doing this brief exercise during the day, whenever you think about it. When you become distracted, simply return to the breath. When you find yourself distracted, gently return to your breath or thoughts. Saying to yourself, "How did I become so distracted?" is simply another distraction.

When we say "working with the mind," there's not so much an actual "doing" as there is "being." We don't do anything to or with our thoughts. We don't try to stop the flow of thoughts, nor do we try to cultivate a blank, thoughtless mindscape. We simply work at being with whatever arises, without following past thoughts, anticipating future thoughts, or prolonging present thoughts. Again:

> We simply work at being with whatever arises, without following past thoughts, anticipating future thoughts, or prolonging present thoughts.

At this point it's important to bring up a point that has been made previously. In order for us to gain some stability in this practice or in this way of being, it's necessary for us to become familiar with our mind. And the only way to do this is to practice, practice, practice. In order for us to be comfortable with this way of being, we need to become familiar enough with our mind so that when it does lead us off into fairy tales, we can gently bring it back. Again, and again, and again.

Summary and Reminders:

1. Our ability to change the quality of our lives and the lives of others depends a great deal on our ability to be present with the world, with others, and with the circumstances—all of them—that life presents to us.

2. The point of mindfulness and meditation is to return repeatedly to the undistracted nature of our minds. We do this by leaving the sensory phenomena within the senses that they arise from; that is, we "leave the seeing in the seeing, leave the hearing in the hearing, leave the thinking in the thinking."

3. What we realize as we work more and more with mindfulness and attending to our minds is that all the phenomena that occur internally—everything that we experience within the perception of our mind and senses—is transitory, ephemeral, and lacking true substance of permanence.

4. Our task in learning to dwell within the compassionate and mindful state of being is to continually remind ourselves that whatever pulls us from our anchor of mindfulness and compassion is temporary, however real it may appear.

5. Even recognizing for a moment that we've become distracted is a step toward the liberation from our otherwise restless mind that spends less time "at home" than we'd ever imagined.

6. Take time, every day, many times a day, to just be with your mind. Mind your mind.

7. Refer to Appendix A, *How to Practice*, for an explanation of the important elements of formal practice.

8. Refer to Appendix B, *Schedule for Practice*, and find the section on working with thoughts.

9. You may wish to go to my website at www.mindingthebedside.com to download guided meditation tracks, MP3s, and other tools that will help to facilitate your practice.

Chapter 6

Mindfulness Is Not Enough

In the last few chapters, we've frequently encountered the terms *awareness,* or being *aware.* I've referred to awareness as being a component of our attending-to, as a way to make sure that our mindfulness hasn't been lost in distraction and inattentiveness. I've also used the words *space* and *spaciousness* to describe an attitude that we should try to cultivate when practicing mindfulness.

Mindfulness, awareness (or meditative awareness), and spaciousness provide the foundation for our compassionate intentions to be directed toward another person, whether that person is our patient or a peer. Lacking any of these components, and especially lacking compassion, the "act" of mindfulness or "meditation" can have a variety of meanings that are not meant for the benefit of everyone. Without the presence of these factors, mindfulness can simply be an exercise in hyperfocus. Being mindful, in and of itself, is not enough.

Take, for example, the skilled cardiothoracic surgeon whose precision in her craft is based on a hyperfocus and attention to performing surgery. While mindfulness may be present in her ability to bring her attention to her patient, there is no implicit fact that she is aware of a deeper abiding aspect of her mind or that she is compassionately attending to her patient. She is simply practicing her trade expertly in a professional manner. Whether or not she is aware of her compassion or even of other thoughts occurring while she is operating may be of no particular consequence in terms of the outcome of the surgery. Her patient will receive expert treatment regardless of whether she is compassionate or mindful of her own intrapsychic dynamics, regardless of whether she goes home and kicks the dog or screams at the kids or of whether she is a beneficent presence or not.

From here on in, when we're discussing meditation and compassion practices, they will have as their basis the three "pillars" of mindfulness, awareness, and spaciousness. These elements are vital to the practice of a meditative presence, based on a compassionate impulse, and are how we work with our mind to insure that our motivation, presence, and state of mind are as clear and undistracted as possible.

The word *meditation* is used in many, many different contexts. There are meditative methods for health and wellness, where everything from relaxation and stress relief to chronic pain and depression are addressed. There are meditative methods for creative visualization and imagery and methods for finding relationships. There are even methods of meditation for attracting money! And, of course, in the context of contemplative and spiritual traditions, there are many forms of meditation—on the divine, on the mind, on God or altruism.

The meditation that we're working with here is based on the tradition of the recognition of a fundamental aspect of one's self that, one could say, transcends even the self. While it is not within the scope of this book to instruct in the methods for realization of this "ultimate" self or mind, the aforementioned three aspects of meditation can bring us closer to revealing this inherent nature of our mind. And as we get glimpses of this more genuine self, we move closer to the compassionate nature of ourselves, the unconditional compassion that we hope to bring to the bedside.

Keeping in mind the inextricable link between the components of mindfulness, awareness, and spaciousness, let's briefly go back to working with the breath and see how each component of a meditative compassion fit into the picture. This exercise will exemplify what is meant by each of the three components. As in previous exercises, you may read the script in the book or use Track #6, "Mindfulness, Awareness, and Spaciousness in Meditation," available for download from my website.

> We'll begin, as we've done in the previous exercises, by stilling our body, sitting upright on a chair, couch, or cushion. Keeping the spine straight, breathe out a long exhalation and, as you do, allow your body and mind to relax. Simply relax into this moment, whether it's for three minutes or twenty minutes. Give yourself a timeout, open up space within your mind, and free it from any constrictions that you may feel. If you're feeling particular stress or tension anywhere in your body, breathe it out, let it go.
>
> Become mindful of your breathing and attentively

maintain that mindfulness with awareness. When your attention strays from your breath, using the awareness of watching your mind, bring your mindfulness back gently and without comment or critique. Maintain a sense of humor, what we could call a spacious humor, about it all. Spaciousness is about allowing this mindfulness to engage all that enters your field of awareness without concern for good or bad, distracted or undistracted.

Continue to practice this way for a while. Just mindfully watching the breath, maintaining awareness of when you become distracted and spaciously bringing the mind back to the breath.

Once you've settled into your meditation, begin to notice how you are feeling. Is there anything about the quality of your mind now or about how you feel that feels different from how you normally are? Is there any sense of well-being, being "good in your skin," that you feel? Are you more at peace with the thoughts as they arise? If you could, would you wish your sense of well-being, either now or at some other time, to be available to those who you care for? Does your sense of well-being affect how you care for others?

Continue to practice, noticing which quality may be strongest or lacking, not criticizing or analyzing what you're doing. Just notice. Practice. And then drop the method, and simply remain in a state of calm abiding.

How was that? Were you able to remain undistracted, simply watching the breath for five minutes? For one minute? Simply watching the breath without any distraction? Aware of your mindfulness? Spaciously bringing the mind back?

Addressing the particular importance of mindfulness, James Austin writes that:

Mindfulness involves attending to the processes of dressing and undressing. It is a steady, persistent returning to a simple mental focus, time after time. Try it. You'll find that you must first set aside a lifetime of mind-wandering habits. Only slowly does the background noise level fall, both internally and externally. With long practice, the advanced meditator develops enough clear mental space to be conscious of each percept individually. With no thoughts. [27]

The lifetime of mind-wandering habits is why we begin to work with mindfulness, to bring our attention to the present moment and to the life that we're engaged in. However, just attending mindfully is not enough. The reason we become distracted and stay in the distraction of our thoughts, emotions, or sensations – even while practicing mindfulness – is that, while being mindful, we lose awareness of the fact that we have become distracted. Reflecting on the previous quote from Joseph Goldstein, we find that while trying to remain mindful, without awareness, we "hop a train of association not knowing that we have hopped on."[28] We may be mindful of our breath or of the thoughts that are arising, but if we lose awareness that we are being mindful, then we become lost. This is the most basic explanation of why we need awareness. In this sense, awareness is the most important piece of meditation; without it, we can't hope to maintain the mindfulness and spaciousness that we'll need to prevent ourselves from becoming distracted.

Of this awareness, Joseph Goldstein writes:

> Awareness is immanent, and infinitely available, but it is camouflaged, like a shy animal. It usually requires some degree of effort and stillness if not stealth to catch a glimpse of it, no less get a sustained look, even though it may be entirely out in the open. You have to be alert, curious, motivated to see it. With awareness, you have to be willing to let the knowing of it come to you, to invite it in, silently and skillfully in the midst of whatever you are thinking or experiencing.[29]

Awareness is immanent, it is always present within the mind. It is the watcher of the mindfulness, similar to what is sometimes known in psychology as metacognition or meta-awareness. It is the cognizance that oversees our thoughts and the processes that occur within our mind. It is the recognition even now that is aware that you are reading and that you are thinking about what you are reading. It is the vital component of mindfulness that insures that we are not falling into a mindful dullness of thoughts without realizing that we are in fact becoming distracted. And it is vital. It brightens our mindfulness and brings about the quality of not just focus, but of meditation and nondistraction.

DROP A PEBBLE INTO A CUP,
WAVES AND TURBULENCE ARISE.
DROP A PEBBLE INTO A LAKE,
BARELY A RIPPLE.

Spaciousness describes the attitude that we adopt or come to realize as we're practicing the art of mindfulness and meditation. It is what allows us to repeatedly come back to our focus, whether that focus is on our patient or our driving. Like the difference between water in a cup and water in a lake, it is what allows all manner of phenomena to arise without creating too much turbulence.

Spaciousness is also what allows us to be present and meditative with compassion for ourselves and for the process. Remembering the quote from James Finley in the beginning of Chapter 4, "We realize we are catching ourselves in the act of perpetuating violence towards our wandering mind, our wayward will, or our sleepiness—in short, toward those very aspects of our self that need to be loved the most;"[30] it is a "loving" spaciousness that we apply to our mind, or if the word *love* doesn't ring true, we could say that we provide a compassionate space within which to learn the art of meditation and a compassionate presence.

Spaciousness does not mean spaced out. It's not about losing one's mind in space, becoming dull or spacey. It's equally an attitude of allowance of all that arises without tightening the mind around the process of mindfully, with awareness, attending to the present moment. Spaciousness is like the sky, the skylike nature of our mind, which holds our mindfulness and awareness. It is not separate from these two but intertwined and equally a part of them.

In a profound statement about meditation and space, the late J. Krishnamurti wrote the following somewhat complex and involved but nonetheless expansive statement about spaciousness and how it relates to meditation. It may give you a lot to reflect on and to use in your practice:

> Thought cannot conceive or formulate to itself the nature of space. Whatever it formulates has within it the limitation of its own boundaries. This is not the space which meditation comes upon. Thought has always a horizon. The meditative mind has no horizon. The mind cannot go from the limited to the immense, nor can it transform the limited into the limitless. The one has to cease for the other to be. Meditation is opening the door into spaciousness which cannot be imagined or speculated upon. Thought is the center round which there is the space of idea, and this space can be expanded by further

ideas. But such expansion through stimulation in any form is not the spaciousness in which there is no center. Meditation is the understanding of this center and so going beyond it. Silence and spaciousness go together. The immensity of silence is the immensity of the mind in which a center does not exist. The perception of this space and silence is not of thought. Thought can perceive only its own projection, and the recognition of it is its own frontier. (*The Only Revolution.* Victor Gollancz: London, 1970, p. 40)

What do mindfulness, awareness, and spaciousness mean to you and to your practice in nursing and in a meditative compassion? Mindfulness may mean sitting at the bedside of someone who is hallucinating and having the presence to help them through their experience. Awareness may mean being able to be present during a "code" without losing one's mindfulness that the person who you're resuscitating is a human being and needs to be treated that way, even during a code. Spaciousness may mean being able to humorously entertain the fact that you've lost your mindfulness after being threatened by an elderly woman with Alzheimer's disease. Or these components of meditation may mean something completely different to each one of us; that's the beauty of the practice. The point is that each of these components is an aspect of a meditative presence that can be practiced together as a unified practice and that can also be practiced individually.

When we envision mindfulness at work, we may picture being able to be more attentive to the immediacy of the situations that our patients find themselves in or able to remain undistracted during a critical period when all of our attention needs to be focused on what's happening. Awareness at work is what brings us back to our patients and to the moment when something not relevant to the present moment pulls us away from the bedside. It's what we use all of the time when managing multiple tasks for multiple patients. When we think about spaciousness while at work, we might begin to picture how our work, job-related tasks, and the challenges that we face at work might change if we apply an open mind to them. Imagine how we might handle difficult situations that arise with our patients if we can allow more space in problem-solving, bringing new and creative solutions to patient care and workflow.

A wonderful metaphor that's often used to describe the characteristics of the meditative mind when it is undistracted, clear and spacious, is that of a candle used to illuminate a picture in the darkness. In order for a candle to light up the picture in the dark, it must be still, because a wavering flame will blur and distort the picture. Additionally, it must also be bright, because just having a still flame may not illuminate the entire picture. Finally, this candle must also be free from obstructions that limit its ability to illuminate the picture. Imagine the picture to be the true nature of our mind and the candle to be the combination of elements that we refine as we practice. Mindfulness is the stillness of the flame, awareness is the brightness of the flame, and spaciousness is the ability of the flame to be free from confinement in illuminating the mind. Use this image if you find it helpful; it can be a powerful visual cue to working with the mind. While practicing, imagine that the deeper nature of your mind is an amazing picture, perhaps one that you've never studied before, and apply the illumination of your mind to investigate the mind, mindfully undistracted, meditatively aware of your mind, and spaciously observing all that you encounter without any bias.

Before we end this chapter, let's do one more exercise to gain familiarity with mindfulness, awareness, and spaciousness.

> We'll begin, as we've done in the previous exercises, by stilling our body, sitting upright on a chair, couch, or cushion. Keeping the spine straight, breathe out a long exhalation and, as you do, allow your body and mind to relax.
>
> Take note of your mind. When practicing this exercise, do you try to "squeeze" your focus into a narrow space, tightening the "muscle" of mindfulness in an attempt to keep out distractions?
>
> Loosely, spaciously, simply relax your mindfulness and awareness into the space of your mind. This doesn't mean spacing out. Rather, it means keeping an open and present awareness, aware of all the thoughts and arisings within your mind, aware of your environment—sounds, objects, smells—aware of your body and sensations that may arise. Spaciously attend to all of these phenomena without the slightest wavering of your attention.
>
> Mindfully attend to the present. When you become aware that you've become distracted, spaciously—with humor and appreciation for your efforts—bring your mind back to the breath or to the moment.

Simply abide, calmly abide, spaciously, in this moment.

And now, relax. Drop all methods. Let go of all effort. And simply be present, here, now.

Summary and Reminders:

1.   Mindfulness, awareness, and spaciousness provide the foundation for our compassionate intentions to be directed toward another person, whether that person is our patient or a peer.

2.   The meditation that we're working with here is based on the tradition of the recognition of a fundamental aspect of one's self that one could say transcends even the self.

3.   The reason we become distracted and stay in the distraction of our thoughts, emotions, or sensations is that, while being mindful, we lose awareness of the fact that we have become distracted.

4.   Awareness is the watcher of the mindfulness, similar to what is sometimes known in psychology as meta-awareness. It is the cognizance that oversees our thoughts, the processes that occur within our mind.

5.   Spaciousness describes the attitude that we come to realize as we're practicing the art of mindfulness and meditation. It is what allows us to come back repeatedly to our focus, whether that focus is on our patient or our driving.

6.   Practice with the tracks downloaded from my blog, paying attention to and working with the three elements of mindfulness, meditative awareness, and spaciousness. For a schedule for working with this exercise, turn to Appendix B.

7.   While you're at work, find moments when you can check in with your mindfulness, awareness, and spaciousness. See what challenges present themselves, and then spaciously work with them.

Chapter 7

Alone with Our Thoughts

The Guest House

This being human is a guest house
Every morning a new arrival.
A joy, a depression, a meanness,
some momentary awareness comes
as an unexpected visitor.
Welcome and entertain them all!
Even if they're a crowd of sorrows,
who violently sweep your house
empty of its furniture,
Still, treat each guest honorably.
He may be clearing you
out for some new delight.
The dark thought, the shame, the malice
meet them at the door laughing
and invite them in.
Be grateful for whoever comes,
because each has been sent
as a guide from beyond.

—Rumi - *Translation source unknown.*

Imagine a patient alone in her room, recovering from surgery for a newly diagnosed malignancy. With no one around, she's alone with her thoughts—with the arisings, the fears, the elaborations of thought and scenarios that may happen—each a new guest, "sent as a guide from beyond." Her mind, untrained to see each thought as simply a passing phenomenon, experiences one dark thought after another as a threat to her wholeness. She is unable to bring her attention back to the present, back to a stability of mind. Instead of promoting a positive neuroimmunological environment, she is weakening her resolve and building up stories of despair, hopelessness, and fear. She is completely at the mercy of her mind.

We've already discovered how out of control our own minds can be, without the added burden of a life-threatening illness or a chronic condition that robs us of our identities and sense of self. Imagine, as we did above, the patient who has been given no tools to deal with the chaotic nature of her mind, whose thoughts come back repeatedly to her illness and disease. How are we going to help this individual if we haven't learned to train our own mind? Imagine how our effectiveness and presence will calm and benefit her if we have worked with our own mind and if we've achieved a certain degree of stability in our mind. Please refer to Track # 7, "Training in a Compassionate Impulse," available for download from my website.

> With the most vivid imagination possible, imagine a scenario similar to the one above. Perhaps visualize a patient who you've seen or met recently or one particularly memorable patient who you've worked with in the past. Conjure up the patient in your mind; evoke the feelings within your own body that he or she must have been feeling in his or her situation. Let your heart and mind go out to her or him, compassionately, fully present. Really be with this person, allowing yourself to feel their suffering, their sense of hopelessness, their utter despair. Investigate the dynamics of your mind to the best of your ability when doing this exercise.

> Whoever it is that you use as the focus of this exercise, feel the compassion that arises when you think of their suffering, and allow a sense of urgency to arise on your part to do whatever is necessary to help alleviate their suffering. Imagine what you would do if you could do anything to help them. Work with this. If you become distracted, bring your mind back to the picture of this person within your mind. Or use your breath to anchor your attention.

> Once you're able to stay with this for a while, broaden this compassionate impulse to include all those you care for, imagining your own family, your loved ones, eventually yourself, as if you were all suffer-

ing from the same illness, dealing with the same challenges. What would you do if you could bring happiness and freedom from suffering to all those you think of? How good would you feel knowing that you could make a difference in the lives of all those you love, care for, and know? Really imagine being able to help everyone who needed your help and see what that feels like.

Slowly, bring the patient who inspired this exercise into your mind and imagine that you're sending to them the same concern that you would feel for a family member in their position. Then, imagine applying this same level of care to all of your patients, even those who cause you some degree of anxiety or frustration. Imagine caring for them as if they were your most precious friend or family member. They are, in fact, someone's family members. Certainly, they were someone's children.

Now, just relax in this atmosphere of caring. Reflect on how each one of our patients deserves to have peace of mind, to have freedom from the anxiety and fears that an untamed mind can bring. And just relax.

Were you able to feel any kind of compassionate impulse arise? Maybe something bubbling up that said, "Yes, I can help." Perhaps you felt a sense of vigor or energy. Regardless of whether you were able to feel something or had some kind of change within your mind, this kind of compassionate presence that we just invoked is what we are working to develop—a compassionate presence that can feel the suffering of another as one's own. What is the difference between these others and yourself in terms of how they're working with the thoughts and arisings of their mind?

The French scientist and philosopher Blaise Pascal wrote that, "All of humanity's problems stem from man's inability to sit quietly in a room alone." This verse reminds us that being alone with our thoughts, with our minds, can be a challenging situation. Multiply that tenfold or one-hundredfold and that's what our patients feel when they've lost all hope for recovery, when they've exhausted all resources for dealing with chronic illness.

As nurses, we encounter the type of suffering that accompanies an overwhelmed mind, sometimes on a daily basis, and have to learn how to be with our patients while also allowing for the "softening" of our heart to their suffering. Allowing our hearts to "break open" with compassion when thinking of these poor suffering beings is what we develop as we become more mindful and present. As we gain more stability of mind in spite of what may arise or what we may feel, it allows us to increasingly show up at the bedside fully and compassionately.

As we are beginning to see, being alone with our thoughts without getting swept away in the deluge takes effort and perseverance. Learning to become compassionate to another's suffering without the distraction of our judgmental minds is an art that requires practice and vigilance. What we forget in doing this work, however, is that there are an abundance of circumstances and situations in our daily lives that can help us hasten the process of working with our minds.

Instead of retreating into the safety of our secure and happy minds, when we encounter the suffering of another, imagine how much more compassionate we can be once we've dealt with our own difficult minds fully and are able to meet our patients in their experience of their suffering minds. When we open compassionately to their suffering, realizing that their suffering comes from no place other than their minds; when we have begun to realize the transient nature of our own thoughts and the suffering that can accompany them, then when we show up at the bedside, we'll do so from the heart of an awakened mind.

Pascal's quote is profound because inherent in these few simple words is the implicit truth that we suffer because we do not know ourselves. For, if we cannot sit alone with our thoughts, how can we possibly truly know who we are? What is it about ourselves that we cannot allow in? Our thoughts and perceptions, our judgments and assumptions, are all interdependently based upon previous circumstances, ad infinitum. Instead of being truly present with what is, we're constantly reacting to our past histories and to our thoughts, expectations, hopes, and fears of the future. But what if we could in fact simply be with our thoughts? Would we find out that our definitions of ourselves as a smart, right, wrong, good nurse are all passing phenomena? And what if that is the case? Then could we also see that our patients' perceptions of themselves as "sick," "dying," and "in pain" are also temporarily existing states based on the assumptions that things are permanent?

What being alone with our thoughts does, among many other things, is to give us a profound understanding of the inherent impermanence of our thoughts and the "self" that we hold to be static. In fact, who "we are" is a constantly shifting interplay of causes and effects. We feel sick because we have not slept well. We feel happy because our patient just told us that we're the best nurse who's ever taken care of them. We feel sad because we've just lost our third patient of the day. Yet all of these states of mind are in flux, constantly changing, impermanent.

Spend some time alone with your thoughts; it may help you see outside of whatever box you've found yourself in. Remember to have a really good sense of humor as you do this, because you may find yourself laughing at the absurdity of how many different things you think of in a very short time.

If we were to use the metaphor of an old-fashioned movie projector, we can imagine that our attention, the unimpeded cognizance of our mind, is like the lightbulb in a movie projector; its sole purpose is to provide the light to bring animation to the movie. In this metaphor, our thoughts are like the film passing by the lightbulb, dependent upon that source of light for meaning. In this way, our thoughts are made manifest by our ability to cognize; we are dependent upon the clear cognition of our mind to think, and yet that pure source of light (keeping consistent with the movie-projector metaphor) has no involvement with the film. When we gain a greater recognition of the light source behind our thoughts, the theme of the movie becomes less important, almost a phenomenon of the cognitive ability of the mind, a projection on the screen, and not the light itself.

Let's do another short exercise.

> Let's imagine for a moment, as vividly as possible, with all the details that we can imagine, that we've just been given an untreatable life-threatening or terminal diagnosis. Bring as much of the power of imagination into this exercise as you can, really imagining your thoughts about your loved ones, about your life and all of the plans that you have for it. Imagine needing to let go of everything or at least having to put it all on hold while you focus solely on the condition with which you've been diagnosed.
>
> Simply try to stay with this exercise, bringing your attention back to the breath whenever you find that you've become distracted. Each time that you return to these thoughts, renew your imagination by utilizing the feelings that are going through your body; use the physiology of your imagination to

give this exercise some life.

You may find this exercise difficult to do, finding yourself distracted. It may not be an easy thing to imagine; not as easy, say, as if it were the actual reality that you're dealing with. Return to the breath and continue to work with being alone with your thoughts, imagining what our patients experience when they're alone with their thoughts, encountering their mind in the midst of illness.

And now, drop the method, allowing the mind to simply relax in a state free of concepts and ideas.

Examining your thoughts, what do you feel when you think about dying, about losing all that you have worked for? As a nurse, as a health-care provider, you've probably reflected on these thoughts before because you've been gifted with the privilege of being present in the process of another's dying or life-threatening illness. What springs to mind when you imagine needing to be cared for in an end-of-life scenario? Will you even allow yourself to entertain these thoughts? What thoughts do you have about winding up in a hospital, having to be the one cared for instead of caring for?

This exercise can be very powerful if you allow your thoughts to arise spontaneously. Keep this exercise in mind the next time you enter the room of one of your patients. Imagine how they're doing when left alone with their thoughts, and reach out with your heart and undistracted mind to be with them. Inquire after their thoughts: What are they thinking about? How are their thoughts affecting them? Perhaps share some of your own insights with them on the magic of working with one's thoughts.

Begin to imagine now how our patients are or aren't dealing with the instability of their minds. If we, in the relatively unencumbered atmosphere of our home or workplace, continually encounter difficulties when trying to stabilize our minds, what of the 51-year-old man who has just learned that he'll need a four-vessel bypass to prevent dying from CAD? Or the 41-year-old woman at the peak of her career as a scholar, who learns that she has glioblastoma?

As a nurse or as someone in another area of the health-care profession, it is very easy to get into the problem-solving rescuer mode. And, to a certain extent, this serves our patients well in terms of medical outcomes. But it doesn't have to be either/or. We can infuse our practice with a mindful awareness of our patients' and their families' needs that goes deep to the heart of their experience of illness and the suffering that they endure. Instead of leaving them alone with their thoughts, we can apply our skills in mindfulness and meditative awareness, combined with a deep heartfelt compassion, to address their minds and attend to their need for clarity.

What a gift we can give to our patients to be able to sit with them after making a diagnosis, or performing a procedure, taking a history, concluding a counseling session, or even while they're dying, and help them to work with their minds...after we've worked with our own, of course. What a precious moment we can offer them to find ourselves at the bedside, fully present, profoundly attentive to their needs in the moment. Thinking about what you've . been reading in the last few chapters, imagine how you could put all of the elements of what we've been learning into practice in helping your patients deal with their minds and helping them when they're alone with their thoughts.

Summary and Reminders:

1. We've already discovered how out of control our own minds can be, without the added burden of a life-threatening illness or a chronic condition that robs us of our identity and sense of self. Imagine, as we did previously, the patient who has been given no tools to deal with the chaotic nature of her mind; whose thoughts come back repeatedly to her illness and disease. How are we going to help this individual if we haven't learned to train our own minds? Imagine, also, how our effectiveness and presence will calm and benefit her if we have worked with our own minds and achieved a certain degree of stability in our minds.

2. Instead of retreating into the safety of our secure and happy minds, when we encounter suffering such as was described in the aforementioned hypothetical situation, consider how much more compassionate we can become if we imagine what our patients are experiencing, alone with their thoughts.

3. If you can, on a daily basis, simply reflect on the preciousness of your life and the gift of health. Imagine what your mind would do with a life-limiting diagnosis and practice being present with your mind, wherever it may go.

Chapter 8

How Do I Become So Distracted?

How hard it can be to turn our attention within! How easily we allow our old habits and set patterns to dominate us! Even though they bring us suffering, we accept them with almost fatalistic resignation, for we are so used to giving in to them. *We may idealize freedom, but when it comes to our habits, we are completely enslaved.*

Still, reflection can slowly bring us wisdom. We may, of course, fall back into fixed repetitive patterns again and again, but slowly we can emerge from them and change. [31]

—Sogyal Rinpoche, from *Glimpse After Glimpse: Daily Reflections on Living and Dying.*

When we begin to work with our minds and with our attention, what we notice is that we are abysmally not present much of the time. We begin to notice the constant torrent of thoughts and emotions that pervades our mind-space and keeps us anywhere but in the present. Thoughts of the past, plans for the future, regrets, hopes, fears, aspirations…whatever our choice of the moment, we spend very little time in the actual present, being with whatever is now, here, moment to moment.

Though it sounds simplistic, in every moment, at every point in time, we are either distracted or we aren't; we're either solidly here, in the present moment, or we're not. We're either altering the clear nature of our minds with what was, what is, or what's to become, or we're remaining unaltered in our present state of being. What this means is that we can use every moment during the day as a check-in to find out whether we're distracted.

What most of us will find as we begin to take note of our "time spent in distraction," much to our dismay, is that we spend very little time with ourselves, now. As Sogyal Rinpoche writes, what we need to do is to "bring our minds home."[32] It's as if all of the parts of our minds are scattered and there is no one at home. Our task is to mindfully and compassionately bring those scattered aspects of self back into the present; the absentee mind needs to return to the present in order to attend to the moment-to-moment awareness necessary for the transformation of mind.

The greatest challenge to our becoming more mindful can actually be the realization of how distracted we are. We sit down to meditate, contemplate, or bring our minds home, and we end up running from the room, screaming, "How did I become so distracted?" Our tendency, once we begin to encounter our distracted mind, is to chastise ourselves, beat our breast in despair, and lament our inability to stay in the moment.

In fact, the realization that we've become distracted is a positive one. Once we even begin to take the time to practice a mindful and compassionate meditation—finding that we can't even stay with the preset moment for more than a few breaths, finding ourselves plotting, planning, living in the fantasy of our thoughts, in the illusion of our fears and hopes—we begin to recognize this way of being as habitual. Once we recognize our normal way of thinking as simply habit, we may begin to feel some degree of certainty or some power in our own ability to change these habits. After all, it's just a habit to be distracted; that's all! So the realization that we are in fact distracted beyond distraction is movement in the right direction. It's movement toward change. In fact, the moment-to-moment realization that we've become distracted is our invitation to the present; within each moment of distraction is the invitation to return home, to return to our true nature.

Even if I'm a born natural, the first time that I venture onto a tennis court, the chances that I'm going to hit every ball over the net and that I'm not going to send a few balls over the fence or step on the fault line are next to impossible. However, if upon realizing that I don't know the first thing about tennis, I flee the court, discouraged at my ineptitude, there is little chance that I'm ever going to learn anything about tennis except that it takes practice and that I can't do it. If, on the other hand, I take it upon myself to practice my serve for 40 minutes every day, there is a good chance that my serve will become better with repeated practice.

Unlike tennis, our relationship with our minds is one that has been reinforced over many years, and the bad habits that we're so accustomed to have been reinforced by repetitive practice. Therefore, it is highly unlikely that we'll become amazingly undistracted after one month or even one year, although we might! In fact, even after many months of practice, we'll still experience periods of practice where all we want to do is flee our practice spot in favor of the daily paper and a good cup of coffee or tea. Our agonizing shout of "How did I get so distracted?" will become the rallying cry that takes us away from our practice. By the way, there's nothing wrong with the daily paper or a good cup of coffee; being undistracted while enjoying them makes them even better!

It is at the moments when we find ourselves distracted and fall into our tendency to judge ourselves that we need to recognize that even our reactions to our distracted minds are themselves more distractions. Each time we beat ourselves up over being distracted only helps us to maintain our distracted mind and prevents us from freeing ourselves from our ignorance. Instead, what we need to realize, at these very moments, is that the thought, *How did I get so distracted?* is simply one of millions of waves to arise on the surface or our mind.

Imagine this: the very thought, *How did I get so distracted?* is of the same nature—made of the same "stuff"—as the thought, *I want to change my mind for the benefit of my patients.* Held together by the same glue of our attention, our positive, compassionate intent is nothing but a thought that we elaborate on and then give life to as an aspiration. The difference is that we choose to cultivate our altruism versus habitually dwelling upon our struggles. What we have to do is get into the habit of changing how our mind is. In that way, we begin to transform the mind simply by aspiring to do so!

Our goal, then, must be to take all thoughts, whether of becoming the mindful master or the next great movie star, as simply thoughts. Our aspiration to become compassionately mindful should not become the next distracting story that takes us away from becoming so. What? That means that while it's good to have the aspiration to change our minds for the benefit of our patients, if we get stuck in the story of doing so without taking the time to practice just being, then our intention will get bogged down in the story of who we wish to become rather than who we're being. It's almost as if we need to let go of all aspirations in order to realize them, because we're all too liable to become so caught up in our expectations of "accomplishing something" that we end up creating the very misery that we hope to escape.

Instead, when we practice consistently and take very brief moments during each day to bring our mind back from its distraction, then we will gradually begin to get the flavor of where it is that we're "going." And, in fact, we're not going anywhere. Instead, we're returning to our mind that has always been present but that we have lost in our distracted view.

So how do we work with these distractions? It's simple, in a way. We use these distractions as the wake-up call, as the meditation bell, as the bamboo stick on the shoulder, as the whack in the side of the head, as the "hello" to wake us from our distraction. If we remember to return to the presence of our minds *each time that we are distracted*, then we can use the abundant distracters as the very calls to wake up.

The Master Tulku Urgyen Rinpoche put it concisely when he stated, "One hundred distractions in a minute's time; one hundred opportunities to practice.[33]"

Remembering the metaphor of the ocean, the nature of our mind is to have thoughts and arisings just as the ocean has waves. Left on their own, without thinking about our thoughts, they'll dissipate and fade away like the waves falling back into the ocean. It's only when we follow our thoughts or create an importance around them that we become distracted. Our job is to deemphasize the ongoing stream of thoughts and—instead—to rest more naturally in the underlying nature of mind, the ocean of wisdom that also creates waves of insight as well as thoughts. Our task is to bring into clear focus the nature of mind that *just is*, that remains cognizant moment to moment, unimpeded and unstained by the turmoil of the untrained mind.

How do we rest on the ocean of wisdom versus being tossed about on its waves? First we need to experience some degree of equanimity when surfing on the waves; we need to not get flustered when we find ourselves falling off the board and to come back to the center of gravity that holds us on the board of mindfulness, even when the wave of the moment is surging and speeding us away.

Our tendency to take our thoughts as real is what leads us to become distracted in the first place. Let's try a short "thought-provoking" exercise:

As in all of our previous practice, find a comfortable position to be in, even for a few minutes, where you can be undistracted and as relaxed as possible. Start by briefly attending to your breath, bringing your attention back to the breath when you become distracted.

Now, as we've done in previous exercises, focus all of your attention on your thoughts. With a firm determination, train your attention on your thoughts, but do so *without becoming distracted by them*. Whenever you find yourself distracted, you may either use your breath or the flow of thoughts themselves as the object of your focus.

No matter how distracted you become, have a sense of humor, even a little chuckle inside, thinking, *Here I am again, distracted; back to my thoughts...*, and let it go.

DON'T TAKE YOUR DISTRACTION SERIOUSLY!

And then, simply relax. Drop all methods. Allow your mind to settle. And simply...be.

What this exercise helps to reinforce is that, as we've seen in other practices, our thoughts are quite fragile, nonexistent, and fleeting. What we take to be so real is very unreal. What's actually quite funny in a sense is that we become so distracted by phenomena that are, quite essentially, unreal! And because it's actually funny at how distracted we can become by things that are so nonexistent, the next time that we find ourselves hopelessly distracted by the seemingly real challenges of our lives, why not return to the present moment... and laugh out loud!!

On a final note, a laugh at myself to benefit my readers. I remember one particularly trying period of meditation, where every time that I sat down to meditate, I became distracted beyond belief. I was really trying, really! However, no matter how hard I tried, I kept on returning to one recurring cycle of distracting thoughts, ruminating on the same stinkin' thinkin' over and over again. Finally, in desperation, I shouted out, "Help me *cut this chain* of discursive [distracted] thinking!" Whereupon a voice inside my head, in the form of a wise old teacher, said, "Sure, show me where it is, and I'll cut it." At that moment, I burst out laughing; all of the pressure that I felt and the solidity of my thoughts simply dissolved. Of course; why was I so stubbornly holding on to the belief that my thoughts and my way of thinking was something that could be cut? There was no "where" to cut my thoughts; there were no solid objects called "thoughts." They were all a product of my mind, and my focusing on them simply made them more "real," or as real as they could be. I still laugh when I think about how tightly I was holding on and how ridiculously simple it was to simply let go of what I thought was distracting me...and how hard it was!!

Summary and Reminders:

1. Our task is to mindfully and compassionately bring those scattered aspects of self back into the present; the absentee mind needs to return to the present in order to attend to the moment-to-moment awareness necessary for the transformation of mind.

2. The moment-to-moment realization that we've become distracted is our invitation to the present; within each moment of distraction is the invitation to return home, to return to our true nature.

3. Our goal, then, must be to take all thoughts, whether of becoming the mindful master or the next great movie star, as simply thoughts.

4. Our aspiration to become compassionately mindful should not become the next distracting story that takes us away from becoming so.

5. Our job is to deemphasize the ongoing stream of thoughts and—instead—to rest more naturally in the underlying nature of mind, the ocean of wisdom that also creates waves of insight as well as thoughts.

6. The next time that we find ourselves hopelessly distracted by the seemingly real challenges of our lives, why not return to the present moment... and laugh out loud!

7. Please continue to practice exercises using any of the tracks mentioned so far, or simply practice being with your mind for a while. Try to keep the practices fun; that is, be spacious and playful about it. We've begun to see how distracted our mind can become and how easily we can return, again and again, to the present. Have fun with it.

Chapter 9

Who Is Doing the Attending?

I AM NOT I

I am not I.
I am this one.
Walking beside me who I do not see,
Whom at times I manage to visit,
And at other times I forget.
The one who remains silent when I talk,
The one who forgives, sweet, when I hate,
The one who takes a walk when I am indoors,
The one who will remain standing when I die.

—Juan Ramon Jimenez

One of the greatest benefits of learning to meditate and to become more mindfully attentive and compassionate at the bedside is that we gradually discover who we really "are." We learn to release the false beliefs about our cherished identities and begin to experience a more spacious, more dynamic, and more inclusive way of viewing ourselves and of viewing others. The "who" of who we are becomes an evolving process versus a stagnant one—a dynamic and malleable process, ever unfolding and evolving. We begin to let go of the old concepts that we held to be the truth of who we are and begin to see the changing nature of our identities by observing the changing nature of our thoughts, emotions, feelings, and sensations.

In working with our minds, we may even find that discovering who we are is not so much about finding out something "new" about ourselves as much as it is about discarding that which is not really "self" in favor of an already existing presence, unencumbered by the habits and abstractions normally associated with who we are.

As we begin to observe the changing nature of our "whoness," we find that the person who shows up to the bedside is also very changeable and malleable.

One day the "I" who shows up is distractible, and on another day the "I" is next to saintly, while on the following day we find that the "I" that we encounter is the very cause of another's suffering, say that of our spouse, child, or fellow driver on the highway.

The benefits of realizing our ever-changing nature are multiple. For example, if we're not feeling particularly benevolent or giving on a certain day, we can forgive ourselves, realizing that that's not who we "really" are. In turn, if we have a particularly saintly day, we can realize that this too will change and focus more on the qualities that we embodied on that day, emulating them in the future, rather than trying to be the "same" every day. Most important is that once we begin to get an idea of who we are and who we really aren't, we'll be able to more fully see this very same "expansive" self in those for whom we care.

So who is it doing the attending at the bedside? Who is minding the bedside? Who are you right now? Think of a few words that you normally use to describe yourself. How do you usually introduce yourself? Do you assume an identity? Are you a nurse? Doctor? Social worker? Or do you practice medicine? Nursing? Social work? What else do you do? Are you a father? A mother? A sister? A partner? Are you Catholic? Jewish? Muslim? Buddhist? Atheist? *XXXX*-ist?

Or, as the poet Juan Ramon Jimenez writes,

> The one who remains silent when I talk,
> The one who forgives, sweet, when I hate,
> The one who takes a walk when I am indoors,
> The one who will remain standing when I die.

Think of all of the things that come to mind when you identify yourself. And think about identities that you may have had in the past that no longer apply to the present; perhaps you "were" a runner, but your knees don't like it now. Or you were single and free and, now you're a parent and ultraresponsible. Spend a few minutes with this before moving on to the next paragraph. "Who" are you?

What we begin to realize when we start to examine our thoughts, our beliefs, our feelings, our sensations, and our emotions is that we are not an "entity" in terms of being a static individual. In fact, we are extremely dynamic. And when we begin to examine our thoughts and our minds, we'll find within them a microcosm of all that exists. Everything, absolutely *everything* is by its nature of being, the result of an infinite series of causes and effects, impermanent and changing. In the very same way that our thoughts move and change, in the same way that we experience clarity of thought and dullness of mind, in the same way that what was important the last minute is no longer important now, so too, the whole universe is spinning at dazzling speeds, changing, evolving, swallowing up, and spitting out.

Besides our professional roles, there are the myriad other labels and roles that we take on. The list is endless, as are the associated accoutrements that accompany each title. And yet, these titles fail to address who we are at our core, who we are when our minds are still, undistracted, unfabricated, uncompounded. When we begin to experience the quietude and solace, the peace and tranquility of a mind left unaltered, we begin to experience a "me" that—appropriately—defies description.

It is this me, the aspect of who we are, that is "beyond words, beyond thoughts, beyond description[34]" that we may chance to glimpse when we still our minds. It is precisely this "me" who can best encounter another "me" at the bedside. It is this me who will listen, unobstructed by distractions or by thoughts that stimulate a reaction, and allow for the person we're tending to, to really be heard, to be healed in the precious moment of the present. It is the still and undistracted mind that won't have to fumble for an answer but will be able to remain—in the moment pregnant with possibilities—alert to the subtleties of the words and body language of the patient. It is this clear mind that will be able to respond, from the depths of compassion, without pretension, without fear of touching their pain, without the distraction of the next moment, next thing to do, next patient to see.

The very basis of a compassionate and mindful presence is that we remain to the best of our ability, in this moment, undistracted. As we begin to *really get* the transient and changeable nature of our minds; as we begin to realize the impermanence of thoughts, emotions, and sensations; and as we begin to apply this realized wisdom to our world, we'll begin to get insights into the fluid nature of ourselves. We'll find that we don't always have to react as expected in any one situation. We'll find spontaneity in the present, a way of taking the dismembered aspects of who we are and putting ourselves together anew, re-membering our essence.

Remaining unaltered, in the present moment—mindful, aware, spacious, and compassionate—we may find that the solutions to our patients' challenges become more "out of the box" and less based on a formulaic approach to our profession. Because our minds are ever-changing, and because behind this ever-changing mind is stability and wisdom, we may find that with more practice in recognizing our truer nature, we're more able to access what's behind the chaos and respond genuinely from the heart of an awakened mind.

What we also begin to realize, ever so slightly, as we attend to the moment, is that what we believed to be solid is essentially empty of essence. The solidity of experiences, of our thoughts, of the ways that we imagine ourselves to be begins to slide away. Just as the coming sun of springtime melts the snow from the mountains, releasing the springs and rivers, the warmth of the compassion and the light of emptiness that we experience can begin to melt away the rigid, solidified, icelike quality of our experience. What we are left with is the richly *pregnant potential*, like the womb that births all experience: empty in its nature but full in its capacity to birth all matter of thought, experience, and life. By attending to our moment-to-moment potential, we naturally attend to the potential of those we care for.

The danger in experiencing this emptiness of self lies in the tendency to run into the arms of nihilism thinking that since everything is impermanent, nothing really "matters"; that it is best to eat, drink, and be merry, since tomorrow we all have to die anyway. Nothing could be further from the truth, because we are not solely independent of others but are inextricably *interdependent* with one another and each other. What we do affects others; how we are can directly affect the momentary present that another individual experiences. Therefore, far from collapsing our sense of self, realizing this momentary nature of self expands our awareness of interdependence and allows us to be proactive in how we affect the quality of the present, in everything that we do and with everyone that we meet.

What we begin to realize is that the "who" who attends the bedside is dynamic, and that the more mindful we are when we arrive in the presence of another, the more genuinely we can show up and the more genuine is the nature of our compassion. Rather than worrying about what we need to do—as a nurse, as a doctor, as a…whatever—we can be free to be one human being looking after the care of another. We can be inspired by spontaneity, we can lapse poetic, we can be outrageous—if that's what the situation calls for—without any apology. This isn't an unbridled, mindless way of showing up; far from it! By not limiting ourselves to "who" we are, we may find ourselves inspired by a pastoral-care staff member if we're a health-care provider, by a doctor's approach to discussing an illness, by a nurse's way of attending to the emotional well-being of an individual, or—imagine—one human relating to another in a manner devoid of professional acumen—simply showing up as one compassionate individual to another.

Because our mind states are in a constant state of flux, it's good to be flexible in working with a variety of mental and emotional states. During my work in hospice, I came to realize that the labile nature of emotions that I encountered when working with those who were dying were very much like my own transient nature of mind, capable of fluctuating wildly within the span of a few minutes or less. Instead of viewing this lability as a liability, we can use our mental and emotional states as powerful tools for transforming how we deal with change in ourselves and those whom we care for. We can learn to view them as we view the passing clouds in the sky, as simple phenomena certain to change in their form and size. We can observe the transient and changing nature of our thoughts and emotions without getting drawn into the stories that we create around them.

Let's work with some difficult thoughts and emotions. In this exercise, remember that whatever you're feeling is impermanent and that you're the one responsible for bringing the feelings and thoughts into the present and can just as easily let them go. Read along with the script and, as always, feel free to listen to Track # 8, "Working with Difficult Thoughts and Emotions."

> As in all of our previous practices, find a comfortable position to be in, even for a few minutes, where you can be undistracted and as relaxed as possible. Start by briefly attending to your breath, bringing your attention back to the breath when you become distracted. The following exercise may stir up some uncomfortable emotions; it's meant to. Just be with whatever arises, as you have learned to be with the different thoughts that arise within your mind.

> After finding some stability within your mind using the breath as an anchor, think back to a time when you felt strong sadness, jealousy, or anger. Do this in a gentle manner at first, letting the feeling arise slowly. You may find that anger or sadness are the easiest emotions and feelings to invoke. If it becomes too much at any time, let it go and come back to the breath. Take some time to remember an incident or time when strong emotions were present and when you felt swept away or affected by them.

> Now, as vividly as possible, open up more and let this memory flood your body and your mind. Feel

the feelings; let the physiology of the moment enter you to a level that feels like you can be with it and deal with it. Feel what it felt like when you were angry, jealous, or sad. Be with the feelings. Be with the emotions. Remember, become keenly aware that all of this is happening in your mind, nowhere else. In a way, really "get into" this exercise by drawing the emotions that you felt into the present and seeing how dramatically you can affect your present state of mind and body *without getting lost in the thoughts and emotions!*

Remain with this exercise for as long as your are comfortable doing so. Return to the breath if you become distracted. Return to the remembrance of your compassionate nature if you get stuck in the emotions. Return to a realization that everything is transient, temporary, almost illusory and that anything that you may be feeling at present is without substance.

Stay with the exercise for a few minutes.

And then, just relax in the vividness of this moment, dropping all methods, allowing the thoughts to move through your mind without grasping after or following them.

As you may have witnessed in the last exercise, we are all capable of experiencing a variety of mental and emotional states within a short period of time and an event that triggers wild emotions doesn't even have to be recent. I've done this exercise repeatedly and have been amazed at seeing how quickly I can enter into a state of mind that has absolutely nothing to do with the present. Isn't it amazing that when we recount our stories to others of having been hurt or insulted by another person, we can enter right into those emotions...even if it was years ago! And isn't it also amazing that in the present, there is absolutely no substance to those stories except for what we create in our minds?

Who is it who experiences these different states of mind? Is it the "self" that identifies with the transient arisings and perceives them as being good or bad? Who is it who is doing the grasping after thoughts? It's a mind that is used to grasping as a way to affirm its essentially nonexistent existence! It's a mind made up of a habitual way of dealing with what arises, creating "substance" where there is essentially none. What happens when we don't respond to these phenomena in our usual manner, when instead of reacting, we greet them with openness and with the realization that they are temporary waves in the unending nature of our mind?

What we see from this work is that as we become more adept at remaining mindful, aware, and compassionate, we free ourselves of the "grasper" that holds on to different states of mind as being permanent. What we could call the goal of this work is to become less identified with the transient nature of our minds—the thoughts, arisings, sensations—and to become more identified with the spacious, compassionate, and clear nature of awareness.

I have to relate personally that actually getting to the place where past hurts (or joys) don't pull me into the story has taken a lot of work, and I'm still not free from this way of using my mind. It really takes time. What makes it all worthwhile is the calm that I can experience in moments of chaos or strong emotional experience, the dispassionate way that I can observe my thoughts and the intense physiology without getting pulled into it. As we'll begin to see, all it takes are a few times of nonreactivity and evenness of the mind to get us coming back to these practices over and over. *Not* being drawn into the stories can become even more appealing than doing so. And it takes time.

The progression of ideas and exercises presented in this book all have the same aim: letting go of our distractions and habitual ways of doing things and becoming more spontaneously present in who we are. It takes time. All of this takes time. Relax and enjoy the ride. You're becoming more fully aware of who you are, and it takes patience…lots of patience!

Summary and Reminders:

1. One of the greatest benefits of learning to meditate and to become more mindfully attentive and compassionate at the bedside is that we gradually discover who it is that we really "are."

2. In working with our minds, we may even find that discovering who we are is not so much about finding out something "new" about ourselves as much as it is about discarding that which is not really "self" in favor of an already existing presence, unencumbered by the habits and abstractions normally associated with who we are.

3. As we begin to observe the changing nature of our "whoness," we find that the person who shows up to the bedside is also very changeable and malleable.

4. What we begin to realize when we start to examine our thoughts, beliefs, feelings, sensations, and emotions is that we are not an "entity" in terms of being a static individual.

5. When we begin to experience the quietude and solace, the peace and tranquility, of a mind left unaltered, we begin to experience a "me" that—appropriately—defies description.

6. The very basis of a compassionate and mindful presence is that we remain as best as possible in this moment, undistracted.

7. What we also begin to realize, ever so slightly, when we begin to attend to the moment—when we bring our presence into the present, moment by moment—is that what we believed to be solid is essentially empty of essence.

8. The next time you're attending to a patient, do so purposefully. Attend to them with the attention to be present, really present. Practice mindfulness and undistracted attention. Attend at the bedside openly, humorously, and spontaneously.

9. Continue to practice with the scripts in the book and with the audio tracks, using the schedule in Appendix B as an example of the progression of practice.

Chapter 10

Another You

When we enhance our sensitivity toward others' suffering through deliberately opening ourselves up to it, it is believed that we can gradually extend our compassion to the point where the individual feels so moved by even the subtlest suffering of others that they come to have an overwhelming sense of responsibility toward others. This causes the one who is compassionate to dedicate themselves entirely to helping others overcome both their suffering and the causes of their suffering.[35]

- Dalai Lama, from *Ethics for the New Millennium.*

Steven had been admitted to my team on the AIDS unit where I was working. After having been diagnosed with HIV, he had done everything possible to avoid using medications, which at that time were associated with significantly undesirable side effects. For a while, he had done well, maintaining his wellness through exercise; alternative therapies; and the avoidance of alcohol, sugar, and other substances that would have impacted his immune system's vitality. He'd continued working and living his life in a normal fashion.

Gradually, Steven's health deteriorated. Without the HIV medications, his immune system faltered and finally failed. His viral load climbed, his T-cell count dropped, and his once vital body became an unwilling host to myriad opportunistic infections. One after another, these illnesses slowly chipped away at Steven's resolve to have a good quality of life. In a desperate act to end what had become an unbearable series of taxing and relentless assaults on his well-being, Steven resolved to take his own life.

On a Friday evening, Steven wrote a short note thanking his caretakers and expressing his love for his family and—in a well-planned and gallant attempt to end his life—took his stockpile of antianxiety and pain medications. His body numb and comatose from his overdose, Steven lay hypoxic in one position on his couch for three days. Unwaveringly, his body refused to die. When his friends found him, he had spent over 72 hours on his couch. His skin had broken down with pressure ulcers on his buttocks and legs that went clear to the bone. The hypoxia had damaged his once clear mind, leaving him capable of only a few utterances, such as "son of a bitch," "goooodammit," and "yup!"

My job and the job of those I worked with was to make Steven as comfortable as possible for the final chapter of his journey, allowing his body to follow the trajectory begun by the cocktail of medications and hypoxia. What followed, instead, was two months of battles with Steven's family—who had never accepted his diagnosis—to keep Steven alive. It was an arduous and often brutal affair caring for Steven, because he was still experiencing pain and discomfort and could only shout out his limited vocabulary when any of our comfort measures disturbed him. In the end, though, the body and will ruled over all interventions, and Steven died.

I was working the day that he died and was informed by one of our staff of his passing. I went into Steven's room to confirm the fact and to ensure that he was in a presentable state because his family members had been notified and were on their way in. I'd been around—literally—thousands of people who were dying, when they died, or who had already died, and this case wasn't any different…or so I thought. As I stood at Steven's bedside, I was struck with an overwhelming and intense realization that the human being who lay in the bed was none other than myself, that at some point, some day, I would be as cold and as lifeless as this body. I saw my life as a brief flash and realized—viscerally—that there was no difference between this once-alive human and myself. Suddenly "it all made sense" in a way that it hadn't before. I deeply understood that as living, breathing beings, we are all striving for the same thing: a life free from pain and, as much as possible, full of happiness, and someday all of our attempts at avoiding the inevitability of death will fail.

With this realization came a rush of physiological juice into my brain and body. I became light-headed and exhilarated; I was both dizzy and solidly planted on the ground at the same time. After some time of remaining in this reflective state, I staggered out of the room, gazed down the hall, and caught my composure…or so I thought. It wasn't until Steven's aide came down the hall that I realized that I was exuding "something" from this experience. Sharon, the aide on duty, looked at me and asked me, "What happened to you? Are you okay? Why are you smiling?" I guess that I was wearing the experience of having briefly transcended my uniqueness in favor of the realization of how alike I was with the rest of humanity.

Bringing mindfulness, meditative awareness, and compassion into our lives brings not only our presence into the moment but can also significantly reduce our sense of "self" and "other." When we begin to get glimpses into the inherent nature of our mind as being the same as the mind of another—that is, unlimited by concepts, connected or interconnected to some indescribable wholeness—then we can begin to shed our concepts of viewing others as somehow different from ourselves.

While the interdependence of inseparable nature that we all share may sound like it's verging on the metaphysical, there's a great benefit for us if we can at least maintain the motivation and aspiration to view others as not being so separate. Briefly reflect once again on Einstein's quote from Chapter 4:

> A human being is a part of the whole called by us "Universe,"
> a part limited in time and space. He experiences himself, his
> thoughts, his feelings, as something separate from the rest—a
> kind of optical delusion of consciousness. The delusion is a
> kind of prison for us, restricting us to our personal desires and
> to affection for a few persons nearest to us.[36]

The "optical delusion" that we have about our separateness is firmly entangled in the way that we view ourselves in relation to the world and to others. Even after years of having practiced these methods, I find myself at times caught in the intense struggle between viewing myself as "part of" versus "separate from" the world. It takes time, but the process of getting there begins as soon as we create more space in how we view our mind.

As we begin to work with our mind and with its dynamics, and as we begin to get a sense of the fleeting nature of all mental phenomena as well as our thoughts about them, the grasping at a tangible self can ever so gradually fall away. While we may find ourselves left with a less definable sense of self, we may also find a self that is more inextricably entwined with all of the causes and connections that make up the dynamism of our lives.

For me, each time that I can release my preoccupation with my own "selfishness" and look upon another as another me, it chips away at the division within my mind. And nothing seems to help this chipping away as much as a compassionate intention toward another person, based on mindfulness and meditative awareness.

What is vital to remember is that it is *through the mirror of our experience of attending compassionately and mindfully to others* that we gain insight into our own nature. That is, when we bring our mindfulness, awareness, and compassion to bear on our patient, in that moment we gain insight into ourselves as similar in nature in our fragility, in our resilience, and in our determination to be happy and free from suffering. And when we begin to embody and understand this realization, then we begin to thin the veil that separates "self" from "other," and we begin to realize the preciousness of others as "another me." Through seeing others as no different than ourselves—that is, wishing to be free from suffering and to have happiness—not only do we find ourselves moved by the suffering and pain of others, we begin to find within ourselves the desire to make "a sustained and practical determination to do whatever is possible and necessary to help alleviate their suffering.[37]" This sustained determination is the gradual, and ever so gradual, realization that the one who is the "other" is not unlike our "self." In my experience with Steven, it was the spontaneity of the moment and my unintended presence at this exquisite opportunity for mindfulness that allowed me to receive the gift of seeing him as "another me." In fact, we are offered these opportunities at every moment of the day, in every interaction that we have with anyone else.

Read the following quote from *The Tibetan Book of Living and Dying,* taking time to reflect on the words and their importance for how easy it is to practice compassion in everyday life.

> Every day, life gives us in innumerable chances to open our hearts, if we can only take them. An old woman passes you with a sad and lonely face, swollen veins in her legs, and two heavy plastic bags full of shopping she can hardly carry; a shabbily dressed old man shuffles in front of you in line at the post office; a boy on crutches looks harried and anxious as he tried to cross the street in the afternoon traffic; a dog lies bleeding to death on the road; a young girl sits alone, sobbing hysterically in the subway. Switch on a television, and there on the news perhaps is the mother in Beirut kneeling above the body of her murdered son; or an old grandmother in Moscow pointing to the soup that is her food for today, now knowing if she'll even have that tomorrow; or one of the AIDS children in Romania staring out at you with eyes drained of any living expression…Any one of these sights could open the eyes of your heart to the fact of vast suffering in the world. Let it. Don't waste the love and grief it arouses; in the moment you feel compassion welling up in you, don't brush it aside, don't shrug it off and try quickly to return to "normal," don't be afraid of your feeling or embarrassed by it, don't allow yourself to be distracted from it or let it run aground in apathy. Be

vulnerable: use that quick, bright uprush of compassion; focus on it, go deep into your heart and meditate on it, develop it, enhance and deepen it.[38]

Each individual we encounter, every being who exists, wants happiness and wishes to be free from suffering. While this may not always be evident when witnessing others' propensity for self-destructive behavior, there resides within each of us a sincere desire to experience happiness in life. For most of us, this concept is not revelatory; it's almost a priori that no one wishes to suffer and that everyone wants happiness. Yet everyone doesn't always appear to have this as their goal.

How many times have we entered a patient's room to find a scared or anxious human being, open, vulnerable, and asking for our professional help in relieving their suffering. Looking at their chart—history of alcohol and tobacco abuse—we find that their actions have not been consistent with their present desire to be free from their suffering. At least, this is how it appears to us. After all, if they really didn't want to suffer, they would have stopped smoking and drinking a long time ago.

What drives someone to continue to smoke, or drink, or distract themselves from the present is the same underlying dynamic that causes all of us to be distracted, the desire to be happy and free from suffering. As we begin to work with our mind and notice the almost constant distractions that preoccupy our presence, we can see that we each have within us the very same capacity as the hardcore smoker or drinker to be distracted and ignorant of our own well-being. We may pride ourselves on our healthy lifestyle; we may eat well, attending to each substance that goes in our mouth; or we may get to the gym on a regular basis, or at least when we can; we make sure that we get the vacation time that we need, even if it means fighting for it. What we strive for— constantly—is for our own happiness. Yet, all the while, we tend to remain relatively unaware of the doer, of the deeper aspect of the self who is behind all of this activity, always doing to try to remain happy and free from suffering.

When we take the time to be mindful about it, we realize that most of the things that we do in our lives are driven by the urge to feel good. Whether we're trying to be a "good person," care for others, or take care of our body, all of us wish to be happy and to avoid suffering. However, because of distractions, instead of taking the time to bring a deeper sense of happiness into our lives, one that is based on an inner contentment, we distract ourselves from the present and rely on our job, family, leisure time, or any number of other things to occupy our minds. If only the urge to feel good could turn us inward instead of outward, right?

Someone who continues to smoke, even when their health is at risk, is in some way trying to attend to the same needs that we attend to by "taking care of ourselves"; that is, avoiding the dysphoria, the suffering, that goes with giving up something that they are attached to. They're focusing on an outer source of happiness, failing to recognize that they hold within themselves the source of true happiness, a mind free from worry and distractions. Whether it's attachment to a professional image or the need for a surge of nicotine, the basis of the craving is the same: striving for happiness and longing to be free from suffering. Does this sound strange? Can we actually say that attachment to good health and attachment to something that causes bad health have the same root cause? One is based on preserving the ability to function, live, and—especially as a health-care professional—take care of others. The other, smoking, is a self-centered habit that is good for only one thing…making one "happy" in an illusory or physiologically seductive way. Yes, both attachment to good health and attachment to a steady state of nicotine satiation are attempts at maintaining what feels good to us and avoiding what feels bad. This can be a lot to think about.

In his book *Full Catastrophe Living—Using the Wisdom of Your Body and Mind to Face Stress, Pain, and Illness*, author and teacher of Mindfulness Based Stress Reduction® Jon Kabat-Zinn writes:

> Mindfulness brought to our actual behavior may drive home the realization that we can be caught, in our mind and actions, between those two driving motives of liking/wanting (greed) and disliking/not wanting (aversion)—however subtle and unconscious they may be—to the point that our lives become one incessant vacillation between pursuit of what we like and flight from what we don't like. Such a course will lead to few moments of peace and happiness. How could it? There will always be cause for anxiety. At any moment you might lose what you already have. Or you might get it and find out it wasn't what you wanted after all. You might still not feel complete.[39]

When we meet our patients in the throes of their illnesses, whatever they may be, with the realization that they are another "me," wanting to be happy and free from suffering, we enter into a relationship of equality with them. We peel away the layer of "other" from the equation. The way that we remain in this mind of sameness is through being mindful, aware, and spacious, compassionately aware that their needs and ours are the same. And the manner by which we train in these ways of being is once again though meditation.

Once we've gained some stability in our meditation practice, we can begin to practice exercises designed specifically to remove the barrier between ourselves and others. One such exercise that I find poignantly useful is the practice of imagining that we can take on the suffering of others and give to them our happiness. In the Christian tradition, this might be likened to the story of how Jesus died to take on the suffering of humans. In the hero's journey, described in depth by Joseph Campbell, it might be the warrior's journey through a hell-like land in order to bring back to humanity a special gift. An example of such is the story of the god Prometheus. In Greek mythology, Prometheus, hero of humankind, stole fire from the gods and gave it to humans. For this selfless act, Zeus chained him to a great rock in the Caucasus mountains, where each day his liver was eaten by an eagle, only to be regenerated each night and then consumed again the following day. Talk about suffering for the benefit of others!

One practice where we can begin practicing the art of selfless service is in *tonglen* (taking and receiving), whereby we imagine that we're taking on another's suffering and giving to them all of our happiness and joy. At first, practices such as tonglen or Prometheus' daily encounter with a liver-eating eagle can seem foreign to those of us who see life's grand pursuit of our *personal* happiness as the ultimate goal. Why would I want to offer that happiness to another in exchange for their suffering? Why would I want the intransigent alcoholic, embattled in the throes of DTs, to take my happiness while I take on his suffering? Especially when his habitual patterns are clearly at the root of his present suffering?

Wishing others to be happy and being "willing to give them our happiness" is not so much about an actual exchange of one set of fortunate circumstances for a set of unfortunate ones. Nor is it about relinquishing the happiness for which we have striven so hard. Practicing an exercise such as tonglen, or any compassion exercise, is about bringing our mind to bear on another's suffering and on a firm commitment—even up to the point of giving away our happiness—to make a sustained effort to do whatever is necessary or whatever we can to end the suffering of another. It's about realizing that on some level, the minds of those we care for and our own mind are no different; that finding happiness within our mind can help others to find happiness within theirs, even in the midst of a devastating illness or health crisis. It's also about realizing, as we gain more strength in our practice of meditation, that we begin to wish for others what we have found for ourselves: true peace of mind.

What follows is a very brief form of working with oneself to imagine that we can take the suffering of another and give them our happiness. Please don't worry. I've done this exercise hundreds of times, as have numerous other people that I know, and not once has anyone "taken" another's illness. What has happened is...well, more for later. For the following exercise, you may read this script by itself or practice with Track #9, "Tonglen."

Just as we've begun our previous exercises, begin by sitting on a straight-backed chair or couch or on a cushion on the floor. Or if you're taking a few moments during the day or time out of work, simply rest in whatever environment that you find yourself. Since we will eventually want to practice in any situation, ultimately it doesn't matter where we are as much as where our attention is. Allow your body to become still. The back is straight without being stiff; the posture is relaxed, awake, and dignified. The hands can rest gently on the knees or in the lap. Settling into this moment, begin watching the breath.

Now, as in the previous exercise, become aware of the fact that you're breathing. Become aware of the movement of the breath as it flows into and out of the body. Feel the breath as it comes into the body and as it leaves the body. Simply remain aware of the breath flowing in and flowing out, Not manipulating the breathing in any way. Simply being aware of it and noticing how it feels.

What we're going to do is use the movement of the breath as a vehicle to practice giving and receiving. Begin by thinking of someone very close to you, perhaps a relative or someone whose presence in your life brings you significant joy. If you can, visualize this person sitting in front of you. If you can't visualize, that's fine. Just invoke the feelings that you experience when you're in this person's presence.

Now, imagine a time when this person has experienced pain or a difficult situation. If such a situation hasn't occurred, imagine how you would feel if this person were to experience suffering or a significantly challenging situation. Whatever you think of, make sure that it's not so charged that you feel like you're sinking in this exercise. If that does happen, bring yourself back to your breath as an anchor and let go of the exercise for a moment.

Now, beginning with your out-breath, imagine that you're able to "send" this person all of the happiness, joy, and contentment that you have in your life. If you yourself are feeling sad or distracted, then imagine what you need right now, in this moment, and then send these qualities to the person. If it helps you with the visualization of this exercise, you can imagine that all of your happiness, joy, love, and care ride the breath in the form of a stream of light. Or you can imagine a stream of warm air or liquid flowing from you to the person. What's most important is that you have a genuine feeling that you are giving this person the happiness that you most cherish.

Perform this sending exercise for a while, coming back to the breath as often as you need to when you become distracted.

Now, on the in-breath, imagine that you are taking on all of this person's suffering, unhappiness, fear, and other feelings of unease. You can imagine a thick black smoke or fog leaving the person and entering you by way of your mouth or nostrils. As this thick smoke enters you, imagine that it enters a "center" of your self-concern, the place within you that feels frustrated with others, burned out, selfish, or grasping after self-importance. Some people find that imagining it entering the heart or center of the chest works best. Whatever you feel, imagine that this smoke enters that area of self-cherishing and then eliminates your own negativity at the very heart of this self-cherishing. Imagine that taking on the suffering of others naturally alleviates your suffering and actually heals you. You can imagine it melting or dissolving into white or blue light or dissipating, the way that mist dissolves as it hits sunlight. What's most important is to really feel that by taking on this person's suffering, you are not only helping them to heal but are healing all of your distraction with yourself and the feelings that prevent you from selflessly showing up for others.

Perform this taking exercise for a while. And then relax. Let go of the exercise, and allow the focus that you had to simply dissolve into the undistracted space of your mind.

However that exercise was for you, whatever happened and whatever came up for you is perfect. This kind of use of the imagination and visualization can take time to get used to. Even after years of working with this type of practice, I can still find myself wandering into thoughts about the person, concerns with myself, or mundane distractions. Simply return to the breath or to watching the thoughts as you've done in the past. You can even dissolve your thoughts or preoccupations into the breath and imagine them being changed into a concern for the other person. In fact, sometimes when I am most distracted doing this exercise, all that I need to do is change my own self-concern and preoccupation into a preoccupation with the other person's welfare.

The most important thing to be with this type of exercise is spacious and forgiving—spacious with our mind and forgiving with our tendency to fall into self-distraction. Remember, what we're trying to do here is really understand that the people who we work with are similar to us, are "another me," and exercises such as tonglen help us remember this.

Once you've gained some experience with this exercise—breathing out happiness, joy, and love and breathing in suffering, sadness, and sorrow—combine the two into one exercise. On the out-breath send all the love, happiness, and joy that you have, and then on the in-breath take on the suffering of the other person.

There are many different versions and types of this exercise. Once you've become stable in this practice, try imagining yourself sitting across from another "you" and consider that this other self is the part of you who suffers and is in need of healing. Imagine that you—the sender—are completely able to give your other self all of the happiness that it needs and take on all of the suffering that it experiences.

Doing this kind of exercise for our patients, even with one simple in-and-out cycle of the breath before we enter a patient's room or before we enter the door to our workplace, can make an extraordinary difference in how we find ourselves at work. It can help refocus and revitalize our tired and burned-out mind and lessen our concern with ourselves. It's a great way to get refocused and centered in the middle of our most important task of becoming more present in the presence of others.

As you develop a greater familiarity with this practice, begin to imagine doing it with someone who doesn't evoke a great sense of familiarity or fondness, perhaps someone you see on a regular basis but whom you don't know. Once you do this, then you can begin to take this practice to those who irritate you or even who have done you harm. When we begin to think about it, there are many of us who have taken very good care of someone to whom, under normal circumstances, we wouldn't have given the time of day. In the varied arenas of nursing, we may even have taken care of people who could have potentially harmed us at one point or another in our lives. But did that stop us from taking care of them? No. Then why should it stop us from wishing for all people that they have happiness and be free from suffering? And what better way to generate this way of thinking than to practice an exercise from the comforts of home or a familiar place, where we can wish for them the very happiness that we enjoy and wish that we could take away all of their suffering.

Summary and Reminders:

1. When we begin to get glimpses into the inherent nature of our mind as being the same as the mind of another—that is, unlimited by concepts, connected or interconnected to some indescribable wholeness—then we can begin to shed our concepts of viewing others as somehow different from ourselves.

2. As we begin to work with our mind and with its dynamics, and as we begin to get a sense of the fleeting nature of all mental phenomena as well as our thoughts about them, the grasping at a tangible self can ever-so-gradually fall away.

3. Each individual that we encounter, every being who exists, wants happiness and wishes to be free from suffering.

4. As we begin to work with our mind and notice the almost constant distractions that preoccupy our presence, we can see that we each have within us the very same capacity as the hardcore smoker or drinker to be distracted and ignorant of our own well-being.

5. When we meet out patients in the throes of their illnesses, whatever the illnesses may be, with the realization that they are another "me," we enter into a relationship of equality with them. We peel away the layer of "other" from the equation. The way that we remain in this mind of sameness is through awareness, and the way that we train in this awareness is through mindfulness and meditation.

6. As a one-minute practice, the next time you see anyone who is in pain or who is suffering due to life's circumstances, simply breath out feelings of love or compassion to them and imagine taking on their suffering. This can be a great way to remember the practice.

7. Please refer to the practice schedule in Appendix B and substitute Track #9, "Tonglen," for other exercises if you aren't up to Week 10 yet.

8. Throughout the day, practice mini sessions of tonglen, practicing taking on the suffering of your patients and giving them all of your happiness.

Chapter 11

If Not Now, When?

[A]nd in the modern world it has always been assumed…that in order to observe oneself all that is required is for a person to "look within." No one ever imagines that self-observation may be a highly disciplined skill which requires longer training than any other skill we know of…In contrast to this, one could very well say that the heart of the psychological disciplines of the East and the ancient Western world consists of training at self-study.[40]

—Jacob Needleman, from *A Sense of the Cosmos*

Thus far we have learned that by attending to the present moment with mindfulness, meditative awareness, and a compassionate intention—resting within a mind that is calm and spacious in its truest nature—we can bring about a profound difference in the way that we approach our work, in the way that our patients perceive us, in our own perceptions, and ultimately in the quality of our lives.

With their emphasis on maintaining and sustaining present moment-to-moment awareness, these practices remind us to take each precious moment as our practice. There literally is no time like the present to be present! In this spirit, it is imperative to take now as the time to begin to work with our mind. The mistakes that we make with ourselves and with others and our failures to understand and perceive life's circumstances are the ongoing opportunities for us to observe our mind and to make an effort to change the habitual nature of our responses, our reactivity to situations, and our "wish I hadn't done that" moments.

So where do we start? When we think, *right now*, what does that mean? Take this moment as an example. You're reading this book…or are you? Where has your mind been in the last 10 minutes? Are you aware of how many other thoughts you've had in that time? Perhaps something that you read here triggered thoughts of another topic or of something that you want to do, have done, or wish you'd done. So, without a formal exercise as your guide, just reflecting on what you've practiced so far, take the next few moments to just sit with your mind, with your thoughts…

Now, how was that? Were you able to be with your thoughts and with the arising phenomena? How did you respond to what arose? Were there thoughts, ideas, or sensations that you favored over others? Were there distractions that arose that you wish hadn't? What was the nature of your mind? How quickly did you come back to your mind? How much did you berate yourself for getting distracted?

While formal practice and periods of intense practice are the foundation of learning to use these techniques effectively, it's in the simple momentary awareness of the present that we gain the ongoing stability in training our minds. In fact, it is the everyday opportunities for awareness that we have the most abundance of.

In our often busy lives, there is a tendency to say "later" to the things that we most need to be doing now. We buy gadgets, daily planners, calendars, wall charts, and reminders to help us remember all of the events and tasks that we're handling. We attend workshops on managing time, on managing multiple projects, on how to succeed at everything. Do we forget to attend workshops on how to manage our mind? Do we forget to attend retreats where we take time from the busyness of our lives to devote time to working with our thoughts and with our mind? What we forget is to make the time to work with our mind and to remind ourselves that it doesn't require scheduling to do this work. There's always time to work with our mind, because our mind is always working on us!

The nice thing about working with the breath, sensations, and the mind is that they're always with us. At any time, in any circumstance, we can investigate our mind, watch our breath, or scan our body for sensations. It's not necessary to sit on a meditation cushion, light incense, or listen to tapes. We've got everything that we need to begin—here, right now—to work on the journey of exploring our mind more deeply and taming the habitual tendencies that have ruled us for so long.

If we really understood that this moment is the *only time* that we have to work with our mind, if we understood that *every single moment* provides us with the opportunity to work with our mind, and if we devoted even one-tenth of our attention to our mind in the present, how different would our lives be? There is a quote by the Indian saint Ramakrishna in which he urges us to reflect on just these things. It's said that he told one of his disciples that, "If you spent one-tenth of the time you devoted to distractions like chasing women [or men] or making money to spiritual practice, you would be enlightened in a few years."

While it may not be our intention to become enlightened, and while chasing women, men, money, cars, vacations, or free time may not be our distraction of choice, what this quote implies is that we all have the opportunity to become substantially less distracted and more truly present if we devote even a small part of each day to the practice of mindfulness.

So what prevents us from attending to our mind? Why don't we spend all of our waking moments strengthening our relationship with our mind? Habit. It's our habit to be distracted from the present; our education, society, and peers encourage it. These influences don't purposefully distract us from our truer nature. After all, our society and peers are just as distracted as we are. It is simply the nature of our society in general to focus outwardly on the distractions, not as distractions but as a way of life!

Our lives are permeated and infused with different ways to be distracted. From the daily paper to billboards, television, and internet advertisements, we are entrenched in a life that pulls us away from the inner landscape of self, away from our awareness of an undistracted self, in favor of keeping our attention focused outward. And not in an outward manner that benefits anyone in particular. And even when we're focused outward, working for the good of others, where is our mind when we're not involved in the crisis of the moment, not involved in the problem-solving of being a health-care provider? Are we mindfully attending to the present?

Some things in our lives are less "distractions" than those mentioned above; they're integral to our lives. Family, children, friends, social obligations, volunteer work, meetings, household chores, bills, finances… It gets exhausting just thinking about it, eh? These are the very things that we most need to be present for. Instead, because we are not living a life based on non-distraction, when we are engaged in these activities, there are always other concerns waiting for us, and we never get time to just be, not do. Or else, one of these things distracts us from another—we think about our kids when we're at work, we think about work when we're with our kids, we think about ourselves when we're at work and with our kids. We fail to take the time for *being* rather than *doing*; we fail to take the time to simply be, purely be, here, now, in the moment.

Initially, at least until we become familiar with bringing our mind back to the moment, we need to create a discipline around practicing mindfulness, meditative awareness, and compassionate practices, undistracted by other things. We need to create the stability in the mind that will allow us to walk through our lives more awake and more aware of who it is that we are and how we are living. Like any new skill, working with our minds and becoming less distracted takes time. Most important, perhaps, is to recognize the immediacy of now, the present.

I like the quote by Jacob Needleman at the beginning of this chapter, particularly his observation that, *"No one ever imagines that self-observation may be a highly disciplined skill which requires longer training than any other skill we know of."* What a profound way to look at working with the mind, that it is a "highly disciplined skill." I've often heard students in mindfulness classes say that they didn't know that it took "so much work" to become mindful. After all, we actually believe that we are present in our day-to-day lives. And we are…to a point. It's getting beyond this point, a point often obscured by our very inability to recognize our distraction, that presents the question, "If not now, when?"

Now seems like the best time to begin working with our minds. What's the alternative? Tomorrow? Someday? The strange thing is, tomorrow becomes today, and then we're stuck with all of our plans for the day. And "someday," as I once heard it said, isn't a day of the week. So, the present is the only time to begin to work with moment-to-moment awareness, because—in reality—the present is the *only time that we actually have, because we have no guarantee that tomorrow will ever come.*

One more thing about working with the now before we move on: until we truly recognize the preciousness of this moment and of being fully present within it, it's a little too easy to put off until tomorrow what *must* be done today. Part of working with our mind is the potential to increasingly realize the poignant fact that this moment is really all the time that we are guaranteed to have in this life. Having worked in health care for 30 years, it is clear to me that we truly never know when our next breath will be our last breath. Recognizing the preciousness of our birth and the uncertainty as to the hour and time of our death should truly keep us inspired in the moment.

Thinking about the immediacy of our mortality is far from being morose; it's actual. I imagine that there are many people reading this book who have either had personal experiences—close shaves—with death or have taken care of someone who was okay at one moment and on the brink of death the next. This "meditation" on death gives us the gift to realize the extraordinary preciousness of each moment as well as the gift to realize that now is the only time that we have to work with our mind.

Remembering "If not now, when?" can be a powerful tool to bring ourselves back into the moment. Thinking about it, there is no rational reason to answer anything than a resounding "NOW!" When we truly know that we're either distracted or we're not, that we're either present or we're not, and that we can't even begin to know whether we are present or not until we learn to actually be in the present, then there seems to be no sane reason not to say "Now!"

Gaining an insight into the preciousness of the moment is the first way to remind ourselves to bring our mind repeatedly, relentlessly, tirelessly back to the moment over and over and over again. And, how precious is this moment? Whether or not you've worked in a trauma emergency room in your clinical practice, just try to imagine that you're the one being hurriedly wheeled into the ER after a runaway truck slammed into your car. Major arteries are bleeding, lungs are punctured, your lifeblood is seeping away. The immediacy of the moment brings you clearly into your mind. The searing pain of broken limbs enhances the clarity of your attention. In this moment, can you review your life in peace, knowing that you have done all that you were able to do to be present, clear, and in the moment? Can you honestly face your death knowing that you've not missed the most important moments of your life, that you've not been distracted by work, worries, thoughts? Can you go to your death undistracted by thoughts, regrets, remembrances? Can you, in that moment, say good-bye to all that matters, say good-bye to family who you will never see again, who—even in your dying moments—may not even know that they're about to lose you?

Reflect on this for a moment before we continue. Breathe.

It was a quiet night in the ICU. I was working at a small rural hospital in a town where everyone knew everyone else. The only thing that kept the hospital census from being completely "local" was that this part of the state had a steady flow of year-round tourists due to the outdoor environment and local historical landmarks.

On this particular night, we were hanging out at the nurse's station; the respiratory therapist was there, as were the three nurses. The ER physician, a hippie from the sixties who we affectionately referred to as "Buddy," had just made his food rounds; it was his job to make sure that any food (especially chocolate!) in any of the units was first sampled by a qualified emergency-room physician to rule out unintentional food poisoning.

When we were about to start the baths early—it was that quiet—there came the familiar *click* of the overhead paging system; someone was about to announce a code. Finally, a little excitement! "All available personnel to the ER, stat! Repeat, all available personnel to the ER, stat!" In our hospital, such an urgent call for staff was only made when mass casualties or trauma (usually more than three patients in this small community) were coming into the ER at once.

Because there were three of us on, and we had only two easy patients, Jeannie and I jogged down the halls to the ER. When we arrived, we realized what the page was about: the ER was crowded with mostly benign patients who were being triaged to the "wait" queue because of a serious multiple-vehicle accident. Because we were both cross-trained in the ER, we were assigned to the car-accident victims.

Jeannie and I entered the trauma room to find Buddy and two of the ER nurses huddled over one of the patients. Another patient was already covered with a white linen, letting us know that he had died and was beyond rescue. One of the ER nurses looked up and exclaimed, "Quick, the other one's gone. Help us get a line in this one; we're losing her!" Jeannie and I immediately jumped to the feet because neither of the ER nurses were having much luck with the arms for IV access. I was just about to attempt a stick when one of the ER nurses backed up and said, "Oh my God, this is Cindy. Oh my God, this is Cindy!!"

Cindy Webbell was the unit manager of the ICU—a very likeable woman who had worked at the hospital for years and had climbed the ladder of promotions to become the manager of the ICU. Lying on the gurney behind us was the severely crushed and lifeless body of her longtime boyfriend. He'd been thrown from the car on impact and had been hit by an oncoming car.

Suddenly our heads were swimming in the reality that this patient in front of us was "one of us." All of a sudden, I wasn't trying to get a line in a "patient"; I was desperately trying to save the life of a good friend, of a dear woman who I'd shared many a crazy night in the ICU with, a friend of all of my peers, a woman who could hold her margaritas!!

None of us ever expects to be "the patient"…or, perhaps we do. In either case, whenever crisis hits us, it's too late—at that moment—to begin working with our mind. And yet, how many times do we find ourselves distracted, forgetting to have enjoyed even the special, noncrisis moments—a special meal, time with our family, a good conversation, or a good book. How many times have we forgotten how precious our loved ones truly are because we've been distracted by work issues, money issues, time issues…issues! Mind wandering elsewhere, the lights on, but no one home! What a more present life we could live if we spent each moment remembering to be present, to be in the moment.

Begin by scheduling practice times. Write them on your calendar, put them in your planner, or enter them into your electronic organizer. Plan the transformation of your mind.

Again, if not now, when? Without anything else in mind, simply stop all that you are doing, right now, at this moment. Bring your body into a position of comfort and ease, and rest in the moment. Bring your awareness to your mind. And relax…

Summary and Reminders:

1.   While formal practice and periods of intense practice are the foundation of learning to use these techniques effectively, it's the simple momentary awareness of the present that provides us with the ongoing stability in training our mind.

2.   The nice thing about working with the breath, sensations, and the mind is that they're always with us. At any time, in any circumstance, we can investigate our mind, watch our breath, or scan our body for sensations.

3.   It's our habit to be distracted from the present; our education, society, and peers encourage it. Our lives are permeated and infused with different ways to be distracted.

4.   Initially, at least until we become familiar with bringing our mind back to the moment, we need to create a discipline around practicing mindfulness, meditative awareness, and compassionate practices, undistracted by other things.

5.   Remembering "If not now, when?" can be a powerful tool to bringing ourselves back into the moment.

6.   Either on paper or in your mind, make a list of all the reasons for not taking these practices to heart now. See if any of them wouldn't or couldn't be changed if you were more present for them.

7.   Just for fun, refer to Appendix C, *Daily Activities for Practice*, and see just how many opportunities are available during the day when you could practice. Add to the list, make up your own. Challenge yourself to double the list.

8.   Please refer to Appendix A for a discussion on how to work practice into your daily life.

Chapter 12

Research Into Meditation and the Mind

From a recent study published in *Neuroscience Letters* titled *The Effects of Mind-Body Training on Stress Reduction, Positive Affect, and Plasma Catecholamines:*

"This study was designed to assess the association between stress, positive affect and catecholamine levels in meditation and control groups. The meditation group consisted of 67 subjects who regularly engaged in mind-body training of "Brain-Wave Vibration" and the control group consisted of 57 healthy subjects. Plasma catecholamine (norepinephrine (NE), epinephrine (E), and dopamine (DA)) levels were measured, and a modified form of the Stress Response Inventory (SRI-MF) and the Positive Affect and Negative Affect Scale (PANAS) were administered. The meditation group showed higher scores on positive affect (p=.019) and lower scores on stress (p<.001) compared with the control group. Plasma DA levels were also higher in the meditation (p=.031) than in the control group. The control group demonstrated a negative correlation between stress and positive affects (r=-.408, p=.002), whereas this correlation was not observed in the meditation group. The control group showed positive correlations between somatization and NE/E (r=.267, p=.045) and DA/E (r=.271, p=.042) ratios, whereas these correlations did not emerge in the meditation group. In conclusion, these results suggest that meditation as mind-body training is associated with lower stress, higher positive affect and higher plasma DA levels when comparing the meditation group with the control group. Thus, mind-body training may influence stress, positive affect and the sympathetic nervous system including DA activity."[41]

It is my expectation that a chapter on research into the mind will become outdated even before this book is published. This is because in the last several years, the interest in the study of mind-body medicine, mindfulness, and even prayer has blossomed. In the empirical arena of medical and clinical research, fields such as psychoneuroimmunology, neuroscience, and psychophysiology have taken the lead in exploring the territory of the mind and in blazing new trails through the frontiers where mind and body meet, where—in fact—they've never been separate.

Because these fields are becoming filled with new data and models of inquiry on an almost daily basis, and because there are so many great studies being conducted, I will only touch on a very few relevant studies and projects here. Those highlighted here address the dynamics involved in working with the mind that we've been practicing and present evidence of the positive physical benefits that can be derived from working with the mind. For additional resources on many different areas of research, please refer to the Resources section at the end of this book; I've loaded it with references for those inclined to the sciences behind the study of the mind. Another simple and direct way to get an idea of where the science of meditation is focusing its mind is to search the published medical literature using PubMed, Ovid, or one of the many repositories of academic and peer-reviewed articles. At last count, when I queried PubMed for the subject of meditation and mindfulness, I came up with more than 1700 articles.

Because I am not a philosophy scholar or an expert in the field of comparative religion, I can't endeavor to chronicle the course of philosophical and contemplative inquiry into the question of what the nature of the mind is. However, in the context of what I've studied and what I'm attempting to convey to you, it is comforting to know that since the beginning of recorded time, especially in the records of first-person methodology, it seems that human beings have been doing research on the mind. As Jacob Needleman writes, "One could very well say that the heart of the psychological disciplines of the East and the ancient Western world consists of training at self-study.[42]" Because it appears that most ancient societies—including those of Asia, India, Greece, and Europe—spent significant time training in "self study," it is safe to say that for as long as there has been the self-awareness of mind as a phenomenon open to investigative and contemplative practices, there has been research into its nature. It's only within the brief time period of modern science and medicine that scientifically rigorous and empirical study into the nature of the mind has been deemed the "gold standard" of factual knowledge. In fact, even the 14th Dalai Lama, the spiritual leader of Tibet, has acknowledged the importance of working conjointly with science and has cofounded the Mind & Life Institute.[43]

For many of us, as Westerners or as members of a modern society, it reassures us to have a nod from science or from those in the know that what we're doing will have measurable results. While anecdotes and personal stories about the benefits of mindfulness and meditation are too numerous to count, there's nothing like an affirmation from a well-executed research study to move one's mind in the direction of change. After all, much of the nursing and medicine that we practice as a culture rests upon the foundation of evidence-based practice.

What modern science is beginning to discover is that the early pioneers into the investigation of the mind were not only able to experience firsthand the observable dynamics of the mind that are now being validated through research techniques such as fMRI and EEG analysis; these seers and sages were able to pass on this knowledge through lineages of practitioners who to this day continue the art of contemplative meditation and practices. Like mountain climbers ascending the highest peaks or deep-sea explorers journeying to the deepest depths, these individuals were able to access unfathomable regions of the unexplored mind using only the mind to investigate itself and were able to describe what they had found in extraordinary detail and intricacy, oftentimes relying on metaphor and parable as a way to explain the unexplainable.

Through the first-person expeditions into the uncharted nature of mind by these early pioneers, others were able to follow the trails that had been blazed to enlightenment and realization. In fact, when reading some of the texts or instructions from these early "researchers," the language seems remarkably similar in its metaphors to the language of modern physics or neuroscience. And like getting directions from someone standing in a city that you're planning on visiting, when we listen to and practice these methods with sincerity, we can find ourselves within the same territory depicted by the speaker. I've often wondered if when Jesus said, "give unto Ceasar what is Caesar's and to God what is God's," he was trying to convey to us the directions to that divine self that he so perfectly represented.

In the following brief examples of research that has been done or is being done into the dynamics of the mind and the benefits of meditation, the information that I'm providing is about the research not the practitioners. I make this distinction because it can be easy to get distracted by the observance of the practitioner, forgetting that working with and training the mind is what matters most to those of us wishing to transform and realize the great potential of our minds. And while science is important in acknowledging the reality of what others describe, trying to actually accomplish or realize these practices simply through studying them without actually practicing them would be like watching a ballet and expecting to be able to perform the dance by simply having observed it. In the end, nothing advances the first-person science of these methods like the practitioners who accomplish them, and that's us!

At the University of Wisconsin in Madison, Dr. Richard Davidson and his staff have pioneered numerous imaging and electrophysiological studies of the human brain to observe the neurophysiological dynamics of cognitive functioning and emotional regulation, neural substrates of various central nervous system disorders, and the effects of meditative and contemplative practices on neural pathways and dynamics of the brain. Davidson is the Director of the W.M. Keck Laboratory for Functional Brain Imaging and Behavior, the Laboratory for Affective Neuroscience and the Center for Investigating Healthy Minds, Waisman Center at the University of Wisconsin-Madison, and is responsible for many of the innovative inquiries into meditation that have been carried out at the Keck Lab.

The major theme of Davidson's research into contemplative and meditative practices is the observance that something goes on in the mind, or at least the brain, of individuals trained in meditative practices. The "something" that occurs varies depending upon the scope of the study, but a key similarity between his studies of meditation is that the brain of an individual who has a regular meditative practice appears more adept at reorganizing or recruiting certain neural pathways and processes to deal with challenges than does the brain of someone who does not have such a practice.

In a number of studies, Dr. Davidson and his colleagues have enrolled long- and short-term meditators, some monks and other lay practitioners, to determine whether mindfulness and meditation have any observable affect on the brain and neural correlates of cognitive processes.[44][45][46] What Davidson and his colleagues have observed in these groundbreaking studies is that specific regions of the brain responsible for information-processing and emotional regulation can be mediated and modulated through the means of meditative practices. Additionally, by enrolling individuals new to meditation and comparing them to experienced meditators, Davidson has not only shown us that with experience, positive results can increase, but he's also reminded us that with sufficient intent and practice, we are all capable of making these changes and that we can in fact get from "here" to "there."

In one study—hailed as "proving" that compassionate meditation practices were at least beneficial for the practitioner, published in the *Wall Street Journal* and the *Washington Post*, and presented in the proceedings of the National Academy of Sciences in November 2004[47]—Davidson and his colleagues compared a control group of college students with a group of monks who were long-term meditators. The monks had practiced between 10,000 and 50,000 hours over a period of time ranging from 15 to 40 years. What was seen was that the monks produced gamma waves that were up to 30 times as strong as the students'. In addition, larger areas of the meditators' brains were active, particularly in the left prefrontal cortex, an area of the brain highly correlated with processing positive emotions. Gamma waves, thought to be present when there is a unity in function and consciousness within the brain, are usually of low amplitude and difficult to see. Those emanating from the brains of the experienced meditators were easily visible, a phenomenon not seen in the untrained individuals. One description of this phenomenon likened it to an urge by the brain to come to the aid of another based solely on a compassionate focus.

Davidson and his colleagues realized that these results had important implications for ongoing research into the ability of the brain to form new connections and to mediate perception and experience based on training. Previously, the brain had been thought to be relatively static in its ability to change after adulthood. Scientists used to believe that connections among brain nerve cells were fixed early in life and did not change in adulthood. But that assumption has been disproved over the past decade with the help of advances in brain imaging such as fMRI and other techniques. What has been discovered is that the brain is more malleable and able to change. Especially in research being done on brain trauma and rehabilitation, it's been found that the brain has an ability to "rewire" itself, a phenomenon known as "neuroplasticity." Recent research has shown that through intensive training, portions of the brain can be "strengthened." For example, the part of the brain that corresponds to how a violin player will use the hand that fingers the notes on the violin actually grows with training when compared with the bow hand, and this growth occurs even if the musician starts playing as an adult. The work with the monks suggested that this potential for growth and change might occur in the emotional centers of the brain as well.

Additionally, Davidson and his colleagues found that when requested to meditate on compassion, the monks were able to generate remarkable brain waves. Perhaps these meditators had attained an intensely compassionate state of mind. And, if this was the case, then with "exercise" or practice in compassionate exercises, people could increase their ability to be compassionate. For more information on this and other research done by Davidson et al, I encourage you to visit the website at the Waisman Laboratory for Brain Imaging and Behavior (http://brainimaging.waisman.wisc.edu/) and read many of the free articles that are available for download.

> "Our study provides evidence that mindfulness practice can lead to being less caught up in and at the mercy of destructive emotions, and that it predisposes us to greater happiness. This happiness may be so deep, so much a part of our nature, that it is like the sun, always shining. However, even our strong innate capacity for happiness can be obscured by the cloudiness and the storminess, the weather patterns, so often highly conditioned, of our own minds. Yet, just like the sun is not affected by the weather on Earth, so our innate happiness may remain unaffected by causes and conditions swirling around us in our lives even if we don't always remember that this is so."[48]

Jon Kabat-Zinn—mostly known for his groundbreaking course in mindfulness, Mindfulness Based Stress Reduction® (MBSR)—has also authored and coauthored many articles on the positive effects of mindfulness. MBSR in particular has been used as a template for many studies and research into the effects of mindfulness practices on health and wellness. A cursory PubMed search that I did simply on the acronym *MBSR* yielded over 83 articles. While all of the research done on mindfulness has not been held to the rigorous standards of highly powered statistical analysis, the sheer numbers of studies conducted on mindfulness warrant their inclusion in this discussion. Examples of studies published on mindfulness and MBSR include, but are not limited to, research on chronic pain,[49] child-abuse survivors,[50] cancer patients and their partners,[51] adolescent psychiatric outpatients,[52] ruminative thinking associated with depression,[53] fibromyalgia,[54] and breast cancer.[55] For copies of the abstracts of these studies, please see the notes at the end of the book. I've also posted many articles for download on this book's website at www.mindingthebedside.com. Additionally, you may download these abstracts and many other relevant articles from PubMed or other websites found within the Resources section at the back of this book.

In one particular study—done conjointly by Kabat-Zinn, Davidson, their associates, and researchers at other locations—measurements of brain function and immune response to an influenza vaccine were measured in participants who were new to meditation and who participated in an eight-week training program in MBSR. Not only were the brain dynamics of those trained in MBSR modified, with increases to the left-sided anterior activation—a pattern previously associated with positive affect—but there was also a significant increase in antibody titer to influenza vaccine in the meditation group as compared with a control/wait-listed group.[56] So, not only did the brain respond positively to training in mindfulness, but the "downstream" effects of the psychoimmune functions of individuals were also positively affected.

While the results of research into mindfulness and meditative practices are important in validating these methods, it's important to understand that these benefits can almost be seen as byproducts or secondary endpoints of the practice of meditation. In fact, Kabat-Zinn stresses the importance of not trying so much to remove the source of one's physical and emotional ailments as much as working with the dynamics of the mind that cause such suffering to further impact the well-being of individuals. Many of the articles on meditation also refer to how the physical and physiological benefits of meditative practices are in a way "side effects" of the practices. What really matters is that we come to recognize our deeper and truest nature. The health benefits are a bonus!

As I stated at the beginning of this chapter, the number of studies into mind-body practices and the rigor of the science used in studying mindfulness and meditation will naturally increase as their prevalence in practice increases. As more individuals incorporate mindfulness and meditative awareness into their daily lives and as the value of a mindful and compassionate presence is more fully acknowledged, their presence within the realm of scientific inquiry will increase. And while I can't even begin to touch on all of the studies that have been done and are being done, what I can do is to encourage you to review the literature, if you're so inclined, and delve into some of this science; it's amazing and inspirational.

What's most important for us to keep in mind as we endeavor in these practices is that our practice and accomplishment of what we've learned will impact not only our own lives and the lives of our patients; we will become the "scientific evidence" that proves these practices can positively affect our delivery of care at the bedside. In this interdependent manner, if we find that these practices are beneficial to ourselves and to others, then we owe it to the community of caretakers at the bedside to share our experiences and realizations with others. Not in an evangelical manner but in a way that demonstrates to others the evidence of our practice, not in what we say but in how and who we are. This evidence will be most convincing as we are able to put into practice those methods that increase our presence and compassion at the bedside.

We can and will affect the future of caretaking in its dynamics of mindfulness and compassion.

For those of you who would like to jump right in to reading a book that is exemplary in terms of bringing the meditative mind into science, I would highly recommend James Austin's *Zen and the Brain*. Its size can be daunting—824 pages with footnotes included—and some of the discussions around the neuroscience of the meditative mind have the potential to be difficult to interpret without a substantial background in neuroscience. But the sheer volume of information that Dr. Austin presents in this text is an invaluable offering and one of the finest books on the interface of meditation and medicine that I've encountered. For other books, please turn to the Resources and Bibliography sections in the back of this book.

Summary and Reminders:

1. In the empirical arena of medical and clinical research, fields such as psychoneuroimmunology, neuroscience, and psychophysiology have taken the lead in exploring the territory of the mind and in blazing new trails through the frontiers where mind and body meet, where—in fact—they've never been separate.

2. Because it appears that most ancient societies—including the scholars of Asia, India, Greece, and Europe—spent significant time training in "self study," it is safe to say that as long as there has been the self-awareness of mind as a phenomenon open to investigative and contemplative practices, there has been research into its nature.

3. What modern science is beginning to discover is that the early pioneers into the investigation of the mind were not only able to experience firsthand the observable dynamics of the mind that are now being validated through research techniques such as fMRI and EEG analysis; these seers and sages were able to pass on this knowledge through lineages of practitioners who, to this day, continue the art of contemplative meditation and practices.

4. In reviewing research, it can be easy to get distracted by the observance of the practitioner, forgetting that working with and training the mind is what matters most to those of us wishing to transform and realize the great potential of our mind.

5. While science is important in acknowledging the reality of what others describe, trying to actually accomplish or realize these practices simply through studying them without actually practicing them would be like watching a ballet and expecting to be able to perform the dance by simply having observed it. In the end, nothing advances the first-person science of these methods like the practitioners who accomplish them, and that's us!

6. Scientists used to believe that connections among brain nerve cells were fixed early in life and did not change in adulthood. But that assumption has been disproved over the past decade with the help of advances in brain imaging such as fMRI and other techniques. Researchers have discovered that the brain is more malleable and able to change.

7. Not only does the brain respond positively to training in mindfulness, but the "downstream" effects of the psychoimmune functions of individuals are also positively affected.

8. The physical and physiological benefits of meditative practices are, in a way, "side effects" of the practices. What really matters is that we come to recognize our deeper and truest nature. The health benefits are a bonus!

9. What's most important for us to keep in mind as we endeavor in these practices is that our practice and accomplishment of what we've learned

will impact not only our own lives and the lives of our patients, but we will become the "scientific evidence" that proves these practices can positively affect our delivery of care at the bedside.

Chapter 13

Mind—The Forerunner of a Healing Environment

In a dark place the sick indulge themselves too much in various fancies, and are harassed by imaginings devised in an alienated mind, since no external phenomena can fall on the senses; but in a bright place they are prevented from being wholly in their own fancies, which are rather weakened by external phenomena.

—Asclepiades of Bithynia, ca. 50 B.C.

This quote by Asclepiades, a Greek physician from the first to second century BCE, poignantly evokes the mishaps of the mind that our patients encounter as they entertain their fears with "imaginings devised in an alienated mind." Left alone in the darkness of space—or in the darkness of their minds—they are subject to all manner of things that go bump in the night. The "bright place" that Asclepiades speaks of could be the hospital environs, and it could also be that bright place within the mind where the imaginings of the mind have been tamed and transformed.

Sacred spaces for healing are not created simply by the measurable environment that holds the physical space, nor are they created solely by the aesthetics that mould that space. They're dependent upon the individuals who come to those places as envoys of healing and by the characteristics that these individuals embody. Space is an extension of the mind; its attributes, qualities, characteristics, and points of movement and stillness are all an extension of the mind or minds that create it.

We've already touched on the subject of what our patients encounter when left alone with their minds, subject to the torrent of thoughts and emotions whilst battling illness. But how does the hospital or health-care environment impact this already difficult process? What of the toxicity or mindlessness of an environment left without the measures in place to ensure a meditative awareness and compassionate presence?

Recent and ongoing research into the health-care environment and patient outcomes has highlighted the importance of health-care design.[57] The physical structures and aesthetics of health-care institutions are being taken into account with more frequency and urgency than at any other time in the history of modern medicine. In her eloquent and poetic book *Healing Spaces,* neuroscientist and author Esther Sternberg writes:

> The new frontier in architecture and urban design must take into account the needs of our emotions and the strengths and limitations of our brain's ability to synthesize the signals we receive through each of our senses. It must do this at every level, from small to large, from our immediate surrounds to a global scale. Research must ask *how* the brain responds to built space, and *whether* specific aspects of design affect specific aspects of health. And more research must be done on whether virtual or actual space, alone or as an adjunct to conventional drug therapies, can be used as a treatment for illnesses in which the environment triggers the symptoms.[58]

The idea of environment as being crucial to the process of healing is not new. The concept of healing space is chronicled throughout the course of humankind's attention to health and sickness. Ancient Greece had the *asclepeion* temple at Epidaurus, where patients came to find out the right cure for their ailments. There, they spent a night in the *enkoimitiria*, a large sleeping hall where the god Asclepius would visit patients in their dreams and advise them on what they had to do to regain their health.[59]

The Maidu tribes of Northern California embraced a story of creation whereby a deity named Sweat Lodge, incarnated as a human, prepared the animals for the arrival of humans by giving each animal a name and then turning himself into a refuge where humans could find strength and courage. Throughout many indigenous traditions, sweat lodges have been seen as places for renewal, healing, and initiation. Additionally, indigenous people in South America as well as the Australian aboriginal people have within their cultures the understanding that certain places and spaces are beneficial to the health and healing of those who are ill.

What modern-day medicine has created in the guise of a healing space is the hospital. However, in many cases, these modern icons reflect a disability and need for care and healing similar to those who enter their doors. Rather than being portals of entry into a nexus of healing, they are the departure from life into a place of illness. Indeed, this is why such visionaries as Esther Sternberg and institutions like The Center for Health Design have taken it upon themselves to address these pressing issues.

In his book *Coming To Our Senses*, Jon Kabat-Zinn writes:

> It is also ironic that awareness, intentionality, and kindness may still be sadly undernourished in many hospital settings, especially since these qualities are what hospitals are ostensibly all about. The very word "hospital" betokens hospitality, an honored greeting, a true receiving. But somehow it is still all too easy within hospitals and the stream of medical care, although nobody intends for it to happen, to get lost, to not be met or heard or fully seen, and to not be followed to the point of completion and personal satisfaction. The people themselves can all be terrific, yet the system can nevertheless fail many of its patients.[60]

It is not the point of this book to address the complexity of the hospital as a healing environment.[61] What we need to address is how we as the individuals who work within the modern Epidauran environment can use the power and presence of our minds to begin the process of remolding and reforming the environments of healing that have, for the most part, gone the way of the Asclepian rituals that invoked the healing space.

In the same way that space holds the physical environment providing the basis for its physicality and dimensionality, the mind—through its activity—creates and infuses the environment with the consciousness to support its activity. If the minds of those working within a health-care setting are distracted from their charge of helping their patients, then the fruition of their efforts will fall short of their intended goal of restoring the patients to wholeness. However, when we arrive not only at the bedside but at the workplace with the motivation of transforming our minds for the benefit of all others, then everyone within that sphere becomes the object of our intentions.

How our minds are and the movement toward wholeness that our minds envision will determine how the places that we create for healing succeed or fail. Whether employees feel themselves to be simple denizens of the environment, or integral determinants of its quality will be a reflection spilled into that environment. As health-care providers, we create the "psyche" for the space within the hospital environment. If our minds are absent or distracted, the environment that we create cannot help but be detrimental to the healing and wellness of those we serve as well as to those we work with. However, if our workspace is infused with our compassionate intention, directed by the spaciousness of mindfulness and meditative awareness, then its occupants—the employees as well as the patients—will benefit from that intention.

Research has already shown us empirically that on a unit where nurses are chronically stressed and overworked, the results in the capacity for the patients within that environment to heal and recover are diminished.[62] [63] Additionally, since we already know that chronic stress impacts health there is also a greater likelihood that employees working in a highly stressful environment will be more susceptible to illness and lower levels of wellness, especially where individuals are not encouraged to maintain their health through working with their minds or have regressive policies towards sick leave and absence. Of this, Robert Wicks writes poignantly saying,

> Stress management includes basic elements of which we are aware at some level but do not really "know" at the level of true commitment. When this is so, people who are in intense helping roles pay for this in terms of psychological and physical health—not to mention the havoc it wreaks in the family and on one's necessary social outlets [and patients!]. If people do not pay for it immediately, they do so eventually. The problem with "eventually" is that in many psychophysical disorders in which psychological stress produces physical changes over time, the damage that seems so quiet and reversible initially becomes, after a period of time, more or less permanent. At that point, even when stress is reduced and personal [habits are]…self-care enriched, the physical harm already incurred will have chronic implications for the rest of one's life.[64]

The ramifications of a poorer quality of employee health include higher absenteeism and the inevitable revolving-door syndrome, with subsequent reliance of temporary staff or staff not familiar with the environment. Research has shown that such circumstances increase the likelihood that mistakes and lapses in care will occur.[65]

Because how and who we are at the bedside matters so much, we could say that mind is the forerunner of a healing environment. While mind is susceptible to the thoughts that arise within it, it is also capable of becoming liberated from these arisings, transforming the inner landscape into one of happiness and contentment. So, too, can the intentions and motivations that arise within our minds and that we embody when we are fully engaged in our workplace help to create a healthier and more mindful atmosphere.

Having worked with our minds, we already know that the mind can be the creator of happiness and the creator of sorrow in our own lives. But our work environment is an extension of our minds just as anything that we do in life is pervaded by the habits of the mind. If our mind is healthy, it is more likely that the environment that we create while at work will reflect a positive state of health, a state of presence whereby all factors influencing the wellness of those we are caring for will be attended to. We are less likely to overlook the obvious fault of aesthetics or to skip the illogical ergonomic liability of our workspace if our mind is engaged in our environment rather than being distracted. We are more likely to make the appropriate observations about changes that are needed for our own well-being and for those we care for if our thoughts are not emotionally overstated. Thus, we are also more likely to follow the appropriate channels, address the necessary committees, and be taken more seriously if we feel empowered by the presence of a compassionate and patient-centered mind.

As we continue to work with our mind, what begins to emerge is the sense that our lives have become an extension of our mind training and that our ability to accurately assess our environment and consequently make the necessary changes to create a healing space will be enhanced. In the same way that we can transform our daily activities into the cushion upon which to meditate, the work environment can become rich with the material for growing the presence of our mind. Every interaction, every meeting, every committee and mandatory training will provide us with the "stuff" to work on in terms of training and taming our mind and in transforming our environment.

The inherent difficulty of tending to our mind inwardly while our job description begs us to focus outwardly can be the very circumstance that pushes us to change how we work with our minds. Once we begin to recognize the dynamic tension of our mind training vis-à-vis our work environment, then each encounter that we have at work, carried out in a mindful manner, will be the opportunity for workplace transformation. As we gain more insight into our propensity to focus all of our attention on the outer and begin to bring our mind home repeatedly while at work, the next "logical" step will be to bring this awareness to the outer circumstances of our work environment and, with renewed vigor and attention, bring about change and transformation. When the wisdom of our inherent nature of mind permeates our environment, it will have no other choice but to change with us and to reflect the clarity and the presence that we have come to embody. And—like the process of working with a mind entrenched in habitual patterns, obscured from its truer nature—transforming the health-care environment will take time.

Through my practice of bringing my training in mindfulness and compassion to my work, I've begun to imagine health-care institutions as temples of transformation and to think of those who work within these temple walls as agents of change, mindful and compassionate change. I have realized that by learning to skillfully work with one's mind, a practitioner can not only gain genuine peace in his or her life but can also positively benefit her or his patients, peers, and—ideally—the very institution that provides the environment of care. So, not only should "If not now, when?" be our call to action; We also need to ask ourselves, "If not here, where?" Where else but in the health-care environment, which so desperately needs healing, should we bring our mind to bear on healing? No other time but now; no other place but here.

Taking one's work as the ground upon which to change is the focus of this book. But taking the workplace and its qualities as the focus of our well-trained mind is also a point that needs to be embraced. The urgency of "If not here, where?" means that we accept that where we work is the environment of practice and the belief that our work environment, given enough time, will change as we change. The nice thing is that as we change and our perception changes, we are more able to see the brilliance of our workplace and the potential that it holds, just as we've done with our minds. We could almost say that if we can change how our minds are, then we can change anything!

So, let's take what we've learned and practice diligently. Then, let's change our minds about the spaces in which we work and make the changes necessary to bring about real and transformative change within the halls, patient rooms, and boardrooms of our health-care institutions. Let's not limit ourselves to believing that we can only make a difference in our lives or in the lives of those we care for. Let's remember that a commitment to bring benefit to everyone includes coworkers and really all people who comprise the very fabric of the health-care system in which we work. Let's return the hospitality and hospitability to hospitals and to the institutions that are so vital and that matter so much to the health and well-being of our patients. Why not? It's all practice. If not now, when? If not here, where? If not you, who?

To end this chapter, I want to again invoke the poetic language of Esther Sternberg and borrow from her book a passage that addresses equally the poesis of space and mind:

> We can each, as individuals, do our part. Rather than rushing
> through our busy days without paying much attention to the
> spaces around us, we need to carve out a few moments here
> and there to allow ourselves to be aware of our place in the
> world and its place inside us. We need to allow ourselves the

time to see the sun glinting off the surface of the leaves, to listen to the sounds of silence and of nature. We need to stop and inhale the smell of ocean sale or the fragrance of honeysuckle on a summer's night. We need to feel the gentle touch of a spring breeze. We can do all this whether we are healthy or ill. We need to let these sensations penetrate us, and take the time for the memories to trigger, both good and bad, to percolate to the surface of our thoughts.[66]

Summary and Reminders:

1. Sacred spaces for healing are not created simply by the measurable environment that holds the physical space, nor are they created solely by the aesthetics that mould that space. They're dependent upon the individuals who come to those places as envoys of healing and by the characteristics that these individuals embody.

2. Recent and ongoing research into the health-care environment and patient outcomes has highlighted the importance of health-care design.[67] The physical structures and aesthetics of health-care institutions are being taken into account with more frequency and urgency than at any other time in the history of modern medicine.

3. Modern-day medicine has created hospitals in the guise of healing spaces. However, in many cases, these modern icons reflect a disability and need for care and healing similar to those who enter their doors. Rather than being portals of entry into a nexus of healing, they are the departure from life into a place of illness.

4. In the same way that space holds the physical environment providing the basis for its physicality and dimensionality, the mind—through its activity—creates and infuses the environment with the consciousness to support its activity.

5. When we arrive not only at the bedside but at the workplace with the motivation of transforming our minds for the benefit of all others, then everyone within that sphere becomes the object of our intentions.

6. Because how and who we are at the bedside matters so much, we could say that mind is the forerunner of a healing environment.

7. As we continue to work with our minds, what begins to emerge is the sense that our lives have become an extension of our mind training and that our ability to accurately assess our environment and consequently make the necessary changes to create a healing space will be enhanced.

8. Once we begin to recognize the dynamic tension of our mind training vis-à-vis our work environment, then each encounter that we have at work, carried out in a mindful manner, will be the opportunity for workplace transformation.

9. Not only should "If not now, when?" be our call to action, we also need to ask ourselves, "If not here, where?" Where else but in the health-care environment, which so desperately needs healing, should we bring our mind to bear on healing? No other time but now; no other place but here.

Chapter 14

Ending with the End

The time spent contemplating and studying impermanence prepares us to accept that the body dies. It's just a natural consequence of being alive. While you are alive, it is important to learn how to live in such a way that you can be at ease with whatever happens. When dying, it's important to learn how to die in a way that is not so burdened by anxiety, fear or pain—to learn how to die without dread.[68]

- Chokyi Nyima Rinpoche, from *Medicine and Compassion*
—A Tibetan Lama's Guidance for Caregivers

The Latin words *memento mori*—"remember death" or "remember that you must die"—were used in ancient Rome and in medieval times to remind the people of the imminence of death and the uncertainty as to its hour or circumstances. It was also believed to have been used in Rome during parades for Roman generals celebrating victories or triumphs in battle. Walking behind the victorious general would be his slave, who was given the task of reminding the general that, although he was celebrating his victory, at any moment he could be brought down by defeat. The slave would shout the words, "Memento mori!"

Being present with the end of life may be the ultimate test of the stability of one's mind. Whether it is the death of another or our own death, how our mind is during the process of dying is of utmost importance. If we're attending to another's death, then we owe it to that person to be present and to attend solely to their process. After all, we're with them in the final act of their magnificent play: their life. If we're experiencing our own death and we haven't worked with our own mind, the challenges that we face and the obstacles that prevent us from dying a good death may be many. Therefore, we owe it to ourselves to create stability and peace within our minds, if not for the sake of our patients, then for ourselves and our dying process.

Having witnessed thousands of deaths—good and bad, expected and un-expected—and having seen how the quality of mind at the time of death affects the dying process, I can imagine nothing of greater importance than learning to attend to our mind when we are in the presence of someone who is dying or when it is our time to die. How a person dies and the quality of presence and the presence of mind of a caretaker affect not only the individual who is dying but all those around the dying person, as well. Mind is the forerunner of all experience, and I can think of no experience more demanding of a mind well trained in meditation and compassion than the experience of dying.

Throughout our investigation of the mind and in practicing methods to sta-bilize our mind, we may have encountered difficulties in maintaining our focus due to distractions and dynamics that take us away from our present. When we encounter something threatening to the idea of self and "I," it tends to amplify these distractions, creating aversions that multiply and arise as phenomena of the mind. So, imagine taking such challenges and magnifying them with the dissolution of that precious "I," with the stormy clouds of thoughts and emo-tions that may arise when one is dying.

As health-care providers, if we've been blessed enough to work with the dying, and if we've had the additional good fortune of having worked with someone who has a "good death," we've witnessed the importance and bless-ing of a mind undistracted and at peace at the time of death. But what of the difficult death; what happens to our patient's mind when the circumstances surrounding his or her death are less than optimal or downright frightening? What happens to the mind when it is hedged in by the sleight of hand of medi-cal technology or by the fetters of a health-care system overwhelmed by hu-manity? How can we help our patients work with their minds in the immediacy of the moment that most humans dread and of which no living person lives to tell the tale? What do we need to have present within our mind when we attend to the mind of another in dissolution?

Mindfulness, meditative awareness, spaciousness and compassion.

What about our own death? How does our mind behave when we contem-plate our own mortality? When I was working with the HIV and AIDS popula-tion in the 1990s, I attended a workshop where the facilitator had us imagine our own deaths and write about them. What was particularly poignant about this exercise was that our facilitator had us reflect on two separate scenarios—our most wished-for death and our most feared death. It was the scenario of the feared death that made most of the participants squirm uneasily in their chairs. And it was the discussion on our inability to prevent such a death that caused the most discomfort in the group.

In fact, there is no guarantee that we'll have a "good" death, that all of our family will be at our bedside and that we'll have the chance for completion and closure. While that may be the most probable outcome of our life (at least in our minds), there always exists the possibility that we'll die in an unexpected, sudden, or hastened manner. How, then, can we work with our minds now so that no matter how death finds us, we'll be ready and able to enter into death with a mind free from regret, fear, and distraction. In working with this thought, it is important to reflect again and again on that fact that death is real and may come without warning. There's a Tibetan proverb that works well as a reminder:

> Don't be like the pigeon. He spends all night fussing about, making his bed, and dawn comes up before he has even had time to go to sleep.

Like the pigeon, we can busy ourselves to such an extent with the many tasks of managing our lives that we can completely forget that all of these efforts will eventually dissolve into our deaths; we forget to manage the mind that will usher us into our deaths and into the unknown of what happens after this momentous event.

In the same way that we discussed the immediacy of the present for working with our mind for the benefit of our patients, the reflection on death can bring us that same vivid immediacy and a heightened awareness of our mind and its habits. Whether we have a spiritual practice or a religious tradition that informs our thinking about what happens after death—whether it's a belief in heaven or an afterlife or a belief that nothing happens after death—because we only have the chance to experience death once in our lifetime, why not make that unique experience one in which our mind is at ease, peaceful, and without concerns. If our belief is that we run into the arms of Jesus after our death, why not create a mind ready for that embrace? If we believe that the state of our mind will determine our next incarnation, then it behooves us to prepare at every moment to ensure that we are clear and free from distraction when the moment arrives. And if we believe that we simply return to the earth, dust to dust, then how could we possibly do anything else than to end this brief encounter with life in a manner that honors the chance that we've had to be engaged in this exquisite dance called life.

If we've worked at the bedside of someone who is dying, whether it's in the hospice, hospital, or long-term setting, we've had a chance to glimpse the dynamics of death and how each person's life circumstances and end-of-life environment can affect the process of dying. I can recall countless times when I've witnessed a death and, because I've known the person or because I've worked with the person for a while, I've seen how the state and quality of their mind when they were alive expressed itself during the dying process and at the moment of death.

In the following exercise, we're going to work with our breath and with our mind around the imaginary scenario of being given a terminal diagnosis. If you have ever experienced a situation similar to this that still causes you too much discomfort, or if this feels like it will be too challenging, allow yourself to simply read through the script without doing the practice. If even that feels like too much, please skip the exercise and reflect on your own feelings about mortality, about the end of your life, and watch these thoughts without attachment or aversion; simply allow them to arise and settle again like waves in the ocean. As in previous exercises, you may either use the following script for this practice, or use Track #10, "Working with Dying."

> Just as we've begun our previous exercises, begin by sitting on a straight-backed chair or couch or on a cushion sitting on the floor. Or, if you're taking a few moments during the day or time out of work, simply rest in whatever environment that you find yourself. Since we will eventually want to practice in any situation, ultimately it doesn't matter where we are as much as where our attention is. Allow your body to become still. The back is straight without being stiff; the posture is relaxed, awake, and dignified. The hands can rest gently on the knees or in the lap. Settling into this moment, begin watching the breath.

> Now, as in the previous exercise, become aware of the fact that you're breathing. Become aware of the movement of the breath as it flows into and out of the body. Feel the breath as it comes into the body and as it leaves the body. Simply remain aware of the breath flowing in and flowing out, not manipulating the breathing in any way. Simply being aware of it and noticing how it feels.

> Allow yourself to be with this flow of breath coming

in and going out. Notice the feeling of the breath as the lungs fill with air on the in-breath and deflate as you breathe out, the chest expanding and collapsing. Allow your attention to gently ride on the sensation of each breath, not thinking about breathing, without the need to comment. Simply watching your breathing.

Imagine that you're waiting in your health-care provider's office and that you've been called by him or her to review the results of a biopsy that was done on a suspected tumor. The receptionist welcomes you, asks how you're doing, and directs you to take a seat until your appointment. Something about the way that she greeted you gives you the suspicion that she knows what your provider is going to discuss with you, and it isn't good. Be with this suspicion and all of the thoughts that accompany it. Let your mind imagine what you would be thinking if you were about to hear some bad news about your health.

Now imagine that your provider comes out to the waiting room and kindly escorts you to an exam room. Once in the room, he or she asks how you're doing, comments on the fact that you've come alone, and asks whether there's someone who could be with you after the appointment. Now you know that something bad is about to happen. Feel these feelings and allow your thoughts to arise as you practice this exercise.

In a sympathetic and reassuring manner, your provider informs you that you've got a Stage IV tumor that has metastasized to multiple sites and says in a sad way, "There's not much I can do at this point. There just isn't any good treatment for this kind of disease." Just be with this, feeling what you would feel, watching the thoughts that would arise. Imagine the flood of emotions and thoughts that come when you think about the fact that all of your dreams, plans, and aspirations are going to come to an end. Think about family, about your career, about your hoped-for retirement plans. Allow the experience to take hold of your mind, and simply watch what occurs.

Just be, watching your mind, watching your breath. If you become distracted, return to your breath and to the exercise, realizing that what you want most is to be able to be here right now, with this information. And, just be.

Allow thoughts and feelings to flood your mind as much as you can. This exercise is about working with the mind, so allow yourself to do it in the imaginary realm, where there is no actual threat to your well-being.

And now, relax. Drop the exercise. Feel yourself whole. Feel yourself healthy. Feel gratitude for the fact that the scenario that you've just imagined is not real.

What exercises like this can do for us is provide us with opportunities to work with our mind in the face of an imminent death. Because the mind can erupt in chaos at any moment, even in the face of a much less significant perceived threat to our well-being, taking our mind to its limit of what is acceptable can be a powerful way of training the mind. And death—especially in our culture—can be the most extreme source of mental suffering and disruption. And, because we don't know when or how we'll die, waiting until the "right time" to work with our mind on this subject may be too late.

> In horror of death, I took to the mountains.
> Again and again I meditated on the uncertainty of the hour of death.
> Then, capturing the fortress of the deathless unending nature of mind.
> Now all fear of death is over and done.

> —Milarepa, the Tibetan sage and yogi

Earlier, in the chapter *Alone with Our Thoughts*, we imagined the patient who is alone with a diagnosis and who hasn't had the opportunity to work with her or his thoughts. If for no other reason than to help those we care for deal with the enormity of the life-threatening illness and dying, we owe it to them to connect with our own minds around death and dying. Imagine if we were completely at peace with our mortality, if death could come at any time and we could greet it with acceptance and equanimity, if we had the belief or surety that what we were about to experience was nothing more than the logical conclusion of a biological or spiritual existence. Imagine how we could be with our patients if that fearlessness could be applied to our care for them, in assisting them to make the transition from life to death peaceful and painless.

As a husband and a parent (as of this writing, my son is five years old), I practice letting go of my wife and my son and letting go of my own life almost daily. While it may seem morose, the practice of imagining what my life or the lives of my wife and son would be without each other in it brings a vivid and clear sense of appreciation to my life and to my endeavor to be as clear as I can with those I love as much as is possible. It provides a quickening and heightened vigilance to my practice of working with my mind and of using all of life's circumstances as training opportunities. Taking life as the path to realizing our minds, knowing that at any time this may all disappear, is one of the most profound methods of stimulating a dedicated commitment to training the mind.

In her book, *Facing Death and Finding Hope*, author Christine Longaker writes:

> The dying would like us to relate to them as people who are *living*, compassionately accepting their vulnerability and suffering while still seeing them as whole. We can do this most effectively by having thoroughly prepared for our own death, and by training in meditation which enables us to connect with the innermost essence of our being. Then, when we are by the side of the dying, we will have the assured knowledge that they are more than their suffering, more than whatever is temporarily manifesting on the surface—confusion, anger, denial, dementia, and so on. We can recognize and honor the inherent goodness within each person, no matter how clouded over it might seem at the moment.[69]

What Ms. Longaker captures so well in this brief paragraph is the relationship between our mind and those we serve, between the inner landscape of our deepest nature and the potential that is held within the healing space when working with another. Recognizing the inherent goodness of another could not be more exquisitely pressing for those of us in health care who, because of our commitment to help those who are suffering, must be present in body, speech, and mind.

What I'd like to encourage each of you to do is practice working with thoughts of your own mortality as they arise; allow them to permeate your mind and simply see where your attention goes. Pay attention to what it is that distracts you the most when you contemplate your own death; these are the gifts of reflecting on your own impermanence. As Esther Sternberg writes, "We need to let these sensations [or thoughts of our death] penetrate us, and take the time for the memories to trigger, both good and bad, to percolate to the surface of our thoughts.[70]" We can use the thoughts and arisings that occur in this exercise as indicators of what may be our greatest challenges when we die, especially if we find ourselves at life's end "prematurely." Will we want to hold on to our family, children, spouse, parents? Will we have regrets that we haven't brought closure to a painful encounter or haven't apologized for a wrong that we committed? Will we wish that we'd expressed appreciation just one more time to someone who was important to us in our life? Each of these thoughts are gifts, in that they can direct our minds and our actions to the business of taking care of what is important while we can, in the only time that we truly have—*now*.

If we work in an area of nursing where people are either dying or have life-limiting diagnoses, we can use these individuals as the subjects of our practice by choosing one of the methods that we practiced in Chapter 10, *Another You*, or that are available as audio exercises, and purposefully do these exercises in our minds when we are with our patients. It doesn't need to be elaborate or time-consuming; sometimes just a simple "Oh, you're the same as me, and this will happen to me in some way, someday" is all that we need. It can be that brief, really! The story that I shared in *Another You* about my patient Steven is a good example of the potential power of relating to others, especially their mortality, as not so different from our own.

Working with this type of practice, bringing our mind to bear on others' suffering as well as bringing it home to our mortality, has the potential to bring us great stability and peace in how we approach our lives. The stability comes from realizing that our thoughts are simply that, thoughts. We don't need to be blown to and fro by the winds of thoughts and emotions, even when they involve our own mortality. We can learn, especially by purposefully placing our mind on death, to be spacious with whatever arises.

In the same way that we can derive stability within our mind by "practicing death," we can also find a deep wellspring of peace coming from the realization that, while it is true that we all will die one day and that we don't know exactly when or where it will be, there is a deeper, more genuine nature of our mind that is untouched by the circumstances and limitations of this life. Resting in that peace and in the peace that comes from attending to the moment mindfully, aware, and spaciously is one of the greatest rewards of learning to meditate on the nature of our mind.

Death is not an aberration, not an anomaly, not a sleight of hand by some wrathful god. It is the natural extension of everything that lives. Impermanence is inherent in all that comes together through the interdependence of cause and effect. The gift of our lives is that we *do* have change, chances to grow, evolve, learn, experience. And, with this gift comes the inevitable event of death, a time when all of the causes that held this precious life together are exhausted. But if we have "captured the fortress of the deathless unending nature of mind," if we have glimpsed a part of ourselves that transcends our thoughts and emotions, then death can be simply another state of mind, perhaps one in which we discover "something" else or "some [other] way" when it arrives. While we may not know for certain what awaits us at the moment of death, I can't imagine that having anything but a well-trained mind—resting in equipoise and natural simplicity, free from all elaboration—could be anything but beneficial.

> The stream of human life is like a dream;
> In the morning, it is as grass, sprouting, fresh;
> In the morning, it blossoms and flourishes;
> but by evening, it is cut down and withers . . . .
> Our years come to an end like a fleeting whisper.
> The days of our years may total seventy;
> if we are exceptionally strong, perhaps eighty;
> but all their pride and glory is toil and falsehood,
> and, severed quickly, we fly away . . . .
> So teach us to number our days that
> we may attain a heart of wisdom.[71]

- Psalm 90

Summary and Reminders:

1. Memento mori.

2. Being present with the end of life may be the ultimate test of the stability of one's mind. Whether it is the death of another or our own death, how our mind is during the process of dying is of utmost importance.

3. Mind is the forerunner of all experience, and when we reflect on it, we can think of no experience more demanding of a mind well trained in meditation and compassion than the experience of dying.

4. When we encounter something threatening to the idea of self and "I," it tends to amplify distractions, creating aversions that multiply and arise as phenomena of the mind. So, imagine taking such challenges and magnifying them with the dissolution of that precious "I," with the stormy clouds of thoughts and emotions that may arise when one is dying.

5. In the same way that we discussed the immediacy of the present for working with our mind for the benefit of our patients, the reflection on death can bring us that same vivid immediacy and a heightened awareness of our mind and its habits.

6. Because the mind can erupt in chaos at any moment, taking our mind to its limit of what is acceptable can be a powerful way of training the mind. And death can be the most extreme source of mental suffering and disruption.

7. Imagine how we could be with our patients if fearlessness in the face of death could be applied to our care for them, assisting them to make the transition of life to death peaceful and painless.

8. Taking life as the path to realizing our minds, knowing that at any time this may all disappear, is one of the most profound methods of stimulating a dedicated commitment to training the mind.

Chapter 15

Meeting the Road

Not only have I been given the most precious of gifts of these incredible and priceless teachings, I've also been given the two teachers of chronic pain and merciless insomnia as constant opportunities to practice what I've learned. Oh joy at my good fortunes! It's not that I haven't made every possible attempt at removing these unwelcome guests from my life; far from it. It's simply that after years of wrestling with them I've come to realize the gifts that each one's presence has in my life. My cross to bear, the vertical and horizontal axes of suffering. Like two Zen masters, day and night armed with the bamboo canes of discomfort and fatigue, striking me sharply when I begin to fall asleep to the nature of my mind that is free from suffering. Life and its circumstances, all those around me, the animate and inanimate, are in a grand conspiracy to awaken me.

—From a passage that I wrote in August 2009
while on a personal retreat and while experiencing
a significant amount of sleeplessness and pain.

In this final chapter I am going to share why it is and what it is that keeps me in these practices. For me, I know that there's nothing more frustrating than being told to "do something" or having "helpful suggestions" offered without knowing the "why" of it. In many ways, my approach seems similar to that of my son, Noah. He'll ask *why* to almost any statement and continue with the process of inquiry until reaching an acceptable endpoint, where his curiosity has been answered, a reasonable answer has been provided into the cause and effect of the subject, or until his parents are totally exhausted! In the same way, simply being told that these methods will bring me greater inner peace and contentment and a more aware approach to the world sounds nice, but let me try it first; let me test the mettle of the methods to make sure that I'm not wasting this precious life, running down empty burrow holes.

What I hope to do in this chapter is personalize this book by sharing with you what has worked for me; why it has worked; and how easy, difficult, joyous, challenging, and rewarding the journey has been in the process of working with these methods. I would have been remiss to consider writing this book were it not for my own experience in working with these methods, in putting them to the test not only at the bedside but in my life—with my wife; my son; my spiritual, physical, emotional, and financial challenges—basically, with my life!

While abundant stories of others' successes with these methods abound, I have worked with each one of these practices and methods in my own life; none of the methods that I've presented here have gone untested. None of the times when I've admonished you to endeavor in practice have been hypothetical; I've done each and every thing that I've encouraged you to do, dear reader. And to make sure that these methods have worked for me, I've put them to the test in every difficult situation that I've encountered while writing this book. Like what? Glad that you asked. In mostly but not always chronological order, during the writing of this book, I've encountered the following "opportunities" to put into practice what I espouse in the pages of this book:

- two traumatic head and neck injuries (one in a construction/renovation accident, the other a bicycle accident on my way to work...in the ICU!) with resultant chronic pain and flare-ups;
- surgical repair of my right rotator cuff;
- being downsized out of a position that I had moved across the country to assume;
- having the emergent c-section birth of my son;
- a (second) move across the country with my family to relocate to my present home;
- the entrance into and expulsion from a corporate job in the pharmaceutical industry, and the challenges involved in having to accommodate a reduced wage;
- in the final rewrite of this book, a major reconstructive surgery of my ankle;
- a startup of a new consulting business in health-care advocacy (in process as I edit this text);
- and most notably, the commitment to a seven-year daily study and practice of these very methods, under the tutelage of my teacher, Sogyal Rinpoche.

Each of these events in and of themselves could have given me all of the material necessary to practice these methods and to realize their essence, especially and most importantly my seven-year commitment to these practices. I guess that I am a slow learner or that I needed an extra helping of life to ensure that I would truly "get" these teachings. For me, these challenges have been the litmus tests, the midterms, the touchstone to make sure that what I was studying and practicing wasn't just hypothetical but genuine.

Many if not all spiritual traditions embrace stories and parables of individuals being tested by God, nature, or some force as a way to determine one's actual maturity and evolution. The stories of Jesus, Buddha, and Mohammed have similar allegories depicting the tests that these visionaries encountered in trying to find the truth. Native American tales, Celtic stories, and countless myths have shown us how others who are on the path of life have encountered challenges and stumbling blocks to their progress on a spiritual, psychological, or emotional path.

> Furthermore, we have not even to risk the adventure alone, for the heroes of all time have gone before us. The labyrinth is thoroughly known. We have only to follow the thread of the hero path, and where he had thought to find an abomination, we shall find a god. And where we had thought to slay another, we shall slay ourselves. Where we had thought to travel outward, we will come to the center of our own existence. And where we had thought to be alone, we will be with all the world.[72]

- Joseph Campbell, from *The Power of Myth*

In his many discourses on the "hero's journey," Joseph Campbell, the well-known scholar and mythologist, expounded quite extensively upon the theme of encountering the *skandalon*[73] and obtaining its gift, citing multiple examples in myth and religion where individuals are put to the test to determine their depth and breadth. In Buddhism, this test by circumstances, or "outer teacher," is known as one of the four teachers and in some cases the most direct way of realizing one's try nature.

For whatever reasons, I have encountered my life as it is. I have become intimately familiar with my mind and with its dynamics, with the foibles and frustrations of distraction from the present, and with the extraordinary results of putting the time into my practice if for no other reason than to benefit those around me—my family, my friends, and my patients. And it hasn't been easy. In fact, there have been numerous—thousands—of times when I have wanted to flee from my practice and wallow in the self-pity of believing that distraction was my life and there wasn't another way. At times I've done just that; I've held firmly to the belief that I cannot control my perceptions of the experiences in which I've found myself. I've felt so completely out of control of my emotions that I've actually believed that someone or something else was responsible for how I was feeling and how I was experiencing the world. All this, and...

I've observed with joy as I've pulled myself out of the abyss of loss of mindfulness and regained my footing on the ground of these practices as well as on countless passages and writings from the sages, poets, and mystics. I've watched my mind as it's returned, again and again, to the surety of my practice; held skillfully in a wisdom that has been passed down from one master to another, based on lifetimes of practice and investigation into the nature of mind. I've watched my excuses for not practicing disappear into the wisdom of knowing that when I practice, formally as well as informally, I am the most human and the most *humane* to myself and to others. I've seen resistance to practice disappear, filled instead with the joy in knowing that I am reclaiming my birthright to my truest and deepest nature. I've had ever-so-slight glimpses into an inherent nature, what some might call a divine self or Buddha nature, where grasping at the importance of "me" has dissipated, momentarily, into a presence much greater than myself. And, then once more, I've seen the habitual laziness of my mind and my hesitation to practice arise again.

I've also seen how my patients and those with whom I work have responded when I am (and when I'm not!) working skillfully with my mind. I've witnessed the magic that happens when I meet others at the bedside, mind in comfort and ease, heart open, attention on the person for whom I'm caring. I've seen the magic of being present with another human as they pass from this life into the unknown of death, where the presence of my mind has made a difference in how they've experienced that moment.

I've also been witness to my ordinary life, my daily life, when I am and am not able to work with my mind. I've seen the joys that my wife and son have when I'm able to show up with them, being who I am in its very best. And I've seen the opposite. At times, and this is a sign of progress—so I'm told—I've been a witness to my mindlessness soon after being so and have had to work with my mind around these lapses, invoking the very forgiveness that I would encourage in others. I've had to correct myself when I am distracted and remind myself that even these small steps are progress on the path.

In the book, *Heal Thy Self: Lessons on Mindfulness in Medicine*, author

Saki Santorelli, Executive Director for the Center for Mindfulness, writes about the healing relationship that occurs when the separation between self and other occurs:

> Perhaps our real work, whether offering or seeking care, is to recognize that the healing relationship—the field upon which patient and practitioner meet—is, to use the words of the mythologist Joseph Campbell, a "self-mirroring mystery"—the embodiment of a singular human activity that raises essential questions about self, other, and what it means to *heal thy self*.[74]

This "self-mirroring mystery" is where the rubber meets the road, it is where our mind encounters the world and our life as it is, and it is the fertile ground for revealing our deepest nature. Sometimes it is only by the grace of experiencing life as occasionally out of our control that we learn to find something within our control, to find what is inherent within ourselves and within all beings. Sometimes it seems that when we are actually working on gaining a deeper awareness of something within, we are thrust into the life circumstances that frighten us or that challenge us the most. Sometimes, it is in these very moments when we find ourselves.

I do not know if there has been a time since I began practicing meditation with the nature of my mind when I did not have some nagging part of myself questioning what I was doing. Although I have spent a number of hours practicing mindfulness, meditative awareness, and compassion practices, there has been another aspect of my mind questioning me on whether it wouldn't be better to be learning something that could contribute to my livelihood, increase my scope of knowledge in a particular field, start a business, train for a bicycle race, watch a movie, cook dinner or... The redemption in all of the turmoil that arises while training the mind is that once we have learned to establish ourselves formally within these practices, once we have begun to gain some ground in the process of integrating them into our lives, then not only does the formal practice provide the support for our daily activities, but our daily activities become our practice. Then, with the wisdom that we've gained through seeing the world in a more intimate way, the choices that we make and the endeavors that we choose to follow will be infused with a mind that is mindful, aware, and compassionate.

I know that I have found less distraction in life, which includes letting go of many of the things that used to be so much a part of "me." This letting go of things can feel like little deaths, and at times I've experienced the letting go through episodes of grief and mourning. My habitual way of doing things, of allocating time to seemingly important issues and to generally wasting a lot of time, has been ever-present, reminding me of how stuck I can get in patterns and routines. However, as I've encountered each small death associated with letting go of what has seemed to be so important in my life, what has been "resurrected" or "reincarnated" has been the infinite body of wisdom that was trapped beneath the self-imprisonment of "who" I am. In the process of letting go of who I have thought myself to be, I've found more of who I am. There's a Tibetan saying that through finding our deeper nature or nature of mind, "we lose the clouds but gain the sky." That is, we lose what has been distracting us from the present and has been obscuring our true nature—i.e., the thoughts about who we should be, how we've always done things, what is and isn't right about our lives, etc.—but we gain the spaciousness and freedom to see things as they exist, as they are, as a reflection of our mind.

At some point, words fall short and attempts at explaining something that is beyond words fall into the expanse of the ineffable. For centuries, sages, poets, mystics, and saints have attempted to point to or point out that which is beyond words, based solely on experience. And it is through my practice and experience of brief glimpses of this...whatever...that I have found the most profound motivation to continue. Here are a few attempts by individuals from different disciplines to describe this ineffable quality of the mind:

> Beyond words, beyond thoughts, beyond description. Prajna-paramita [perfection of wisdom], unborn, unceasing, with nature like the sky.
>
> —*The Heart Sutra*, part of the larger Buddhist collection of Prajnaparamita sutras

> The Tao that can be told is not the eternal Tao; the name that can be named is not the eternal name.
>
> —The *Tao Te Ching*

> No one can adequately grasp the terms pertaining to God. For example, "mother" is mentioned in place of "father." Both terms mean the same, because the divine is neither male nor female (for how could such a thing be contemplated in the divinity, when it does not remain intact permanently for us human beings either? But when all shall become one in Christ, we will be divested of the signs of this distinction together with the whole of the old man). Therefore, every name found

[in Scripture] is equally able to indicate the ineffable nature, since the meaning of the undefiled nature is contaminated by neither female nor male.

—Gregory of Nyssa, *Commentary on the Song of Songs*

The particulars of what has worked for me are quite simple though not always easy to remember or to return to when I'm embroiled in life's great drama. For instance, something as simple as returning to the breath when I find myself distracted has been able to affect an enormous change over my mind simply because I've practiced it enough. Having gained enough familiarity with the practice, I've found that—within this state of nondistraction—a sense of peace and equanimity unfolds that is uncomplicated by the thoughts that may or may not still arise within my mind. Again, it's not so much about watching the breath as it is about getting to a place of nondistraction, so that whatever may be occurring within the outer environment or the inner environment of my mind, there is less clutter, less clustering of ideas, less elaboration on my reactions and emotions.

Returning to the breath is the beginning to returning to the mind. As infrequent as these occasions may be, when I *am* able to return simply to my mind, again without elaborating on what I find there, what I experience is a mind that has returned to a nature not bound by ideas, fears, concepts, and judgments; it simply is. Again, I'm not trying to get to a "place" of equanimity within my mind. This state of mind is simply the exquisite benefit of not going where I usually go, of not falling into the usual path of distraction, but of instead choosing a path of clarity. In fact, this state of mind is always present, like the sky behind the clouds. It's not something that we have to create but rather that we uncover from the habitual cloudy nature of our mind. The magic of an unaltered and undistracted mind, the benefit of learning to return home to my true nature, is that I am more of who I "am," that being a compassionate, unhurried, and attentive human being. And I can think of no better way of being than when I am working with patients, when I'm with my wife and son, when I'm with my friends, or when I am engaged with those who I have problems with; really anytime!

This way of being is not a pie-in-the-sky ideal, not a special way that only special people can be. It's not about religion or focus on a dogma. While we may find that we feel more "spiritual" or more connected as we ease ourselves into this way of being, what we find is that we are simply more of who we are, unencumbered by our habits and reactions.

For many years, I traveled on the difficult path of trying to change my mind alone. Not alone in terms of solitude away from people, but alone in terms of trying to do it myself, taking various methods and practices to heart but always relying on the confused patterns of my mind to try to change my mind. In each case, I could find myself coming closer to something else, a new way of being, but I would always trip and stumble on the habitual me that was trying to educate myself out of being so habitual. I constantly relied on a limited mind to try to free my mind from its limitations. It never worked; I always found myself standing short of realizing what it was to truly free my mind. I sincerely believe that this was because I was trying to teach myself something that I hadn't ever experienced. Even if I read books, there was no way for the words to convey an experience to me any more than I could've learned to become a nurse without someone to instruct me on the craft.

It wasn't until I entertained the notion of finding a teacher that I hit upon the crucial element missing in my study and practice. It wasn't until I tired of trying to teach myself new ways of being that I accepted that maybe there are others who know more about my mind than I do. And, for me, it wasn't until I met a teacher in person, someone living, who could say, "Not quite, let me show you," that I actually began to make some progress on this path. There's a belief in Buddhism that only after we've really tried to make change and have had the aspiration to do so for the benefit of others do we encounter the "outer manifestation" of our own wisdom-mind in the form of a teacher. For me, this incredible person presented himself in the form of Sogyal Rinpoche. For you, it may be someone who embodies a way of being that is actualized in how they are in the world, or perhaps someone within your church or within a spiritual discipline. They might be a teacher of dance or music, or of martial arts. Most importantly, before you study with anyone, spend time with them and listen to them. Make sure that what you sense and experience is genuine. Then you'll know that what they convey to you is beyond words and that they're embodying their teachings, that they're walking the talk, and that they're teaching from the very heart of wisdom that they're presenting.

While I cannot admonish anyone else to choose anyone as their teacher, I would not be fully sharing my story in trying to convey these methods to you were I not to at least suggest to each of you that you explore and find someone whose words or methods resonate with you, someone who has truly actualized the practices of finding their inner nature, their godlike self, the nature of mind, their divine self, Buddha nature, emotional brilliance…whatever you wish to call it. And while reading from a book by any number of teachers may fulfill a great deal in terms of gaining insight into how to become more fully mindful, aware, and compassionate, there's nothing like having a person who can find the places where you are hiding from your deepest truth to remind you that you are doing just that.

At the back of this book, and on my website and blog, I've included numerous links and references to teachers who embody these kinds of practices. For example, there's James Finley, author of the book *Christian Meditation: Experiencing the Presence of God*. While I haven't had the opportunity to study with him personally, I find that the quality of teaching that he embodies exemplifies a learned wisdom rather than a theoretical one.

In our culture, it's really easy to say, "If it is to be, it's up to me," and pulling oneself up by the bootstraps is what has given us all an advantage in this world of ours. But just as an Olympic athlete needs a coach who has followed a path toward Mount Olympus or a dancer needs an instructor who knows the actual practice of doing an arabesque, if we truly wish to take on the practice of recognizing the nature of our mind, I can think of no better way of realizing this than relying on someone who has been there and done that.

I invite each one of you to attend to yourselves and to make the commitment to really study and practice the numerous methods of mindfulness, meditation, and compassion that are available to you. Make a concerted effort to take just this moment, and then another moment, to wake up to who you are in your heart and mind. Test it. Try it. Muddle over it and really apply your mind to it. Find and lose yourself at the bedside repeatedly. That's what it's about. That's what this book is for. Use this book as a tool, as a resource. Read it more than once, underline passages that make sense or that you want to know more about. Investigate the resources that I've provided at the back of this book. Visit my blog and website and see what I'm able to do to provide you with more. If there's something missing, contact me and let me know.

Begin the study of who you are; you may find out that you are truly a whole lot more...and less! Take on the process with a sense of humor and adventure, entering into this journey with the resolve to engage the deepest and truest sense of who you are. Try. Fail. Try again. Succeed. Try again. Fail again. Make a joyful life out of realizing that your birthright is to become more of who you are really are each and every day. Enjoy.

This World Which Is Made of Our Love for Emptiness

Praise to the emptiness that blanks out existence. Existence:
This place made from our love for that emptiness!

Yet somehow comes emptiness,
this existence goes.

Praise to that happening, over and over!
For years I pulled my own existence out of emptiness.

Then one swoop, one swing of the arm,
that work is over.

Free of who I was, free of presence, free of dangerous fear, hope,
free of mountainous wanting.

The here-and-now mountain is a tiny piece of a piece of straw
blown off into emptiness.

These words I'm saying so much begin to lose meaning:
Existence, emptiness, mountain, straw:

Words and what they try to say swept
out the window, down the slant of the roof.

—Mevlana Jalaludin Rumi

As a post-postscript, I am already in the process of writing a "next book," a follow-up to this book that will deepen both my process in learning to convey this information to you as well as your process of learning to work with your mind. Not only do I plan on bringing out and teasing out more of the information contained within—expanding the exercises and practices that I have learned—but I want to involve you in how I can clearly present this information. I envision the next book as heavy on the practice side, discussing ways to deepen what has been presented here as well as to answer any questions that may come up from you, the reader. If there is something that needs to be opened more, if you would like to deepen your practice in specific areas, or if I've missed the boat in how I presented this information, please let me know. Thank you.

Appendices:

Appendix A: —How to Practice

As a beginner in any new study—whether tennis, sewing, writing, or piano—what is most vital for a student are the proper environment, the right tools, the correct motivation, and consistency in practicing.

For the right practice environment, what we need is a place and time away from the habitual distractions of our daily lives. Even if these distractions are positive ones—our loved ones, our hobbies, or our professional studies—we've got to carve out a time and place to spend with ourselves.

Creating space for this precious time doesn't have to be elaborate. It can be as simple as a comfortable chair or as elaborate as a nook in a room, set up with a shrine or altar with sacred objects, such as pictures, flowers, or important reminders of a particular spiritual tradition. What's most important is to not become so fixated on creating the space that you forsake the time. For myself, although I have a particular place in my home set aside for my practice, on many—and sometimes most—occasions, I wake up, pull my pillow up between my back and the headboard, and practice, even before I get up to start my day. Actually, practicing like this, taking time when you immediately wake up, can be a great reminder to begin your day in a space of mindful, meditative, and compassionate presence.

The time that we practice needs to be open and spacious enough to allow us freedom to focus on what we're practicing without thoughts of what we need to do next, what we're not doing now, or any number of invasive thoughts that—almost guaranteed—will arise anyway. The time needs to be "our time," a time when we give to ourselves the precious opportunity to work with our mind and discover a stillness, a calm abiding nature, that will benefit us throughout our busy daily schedule, adding to our ability to be in the moment to truly enjoy what matters most.

In Appendix B, I've provided a sample of a schedule that you can use to get into gear and into the habit of practice. It's not fixed, it's not a "must," it's simply one way of creating the discipline necessary to succeed in learning the practices of mindfulness, meditative awareness, and compassion. What is most important, what is vital, and what is almost "non-negotiable" is that you commit to consistently working with these techniques for at least 12 weeks. Why 12 weeks? Because after 12 weeks, you'll have become familiar enough with the methods and techniques to see some progress and some benefit. And because—hopefully—you'll have created enough of a routine so that the habits of not attending to your mind will have become somewhat, *somewhat,* replaced by the routine of attending to your mind.

Taking the time is up to you, so in that sense, of course it's negotiable. Yet, as was stated in the line "If not now, when?" there will be no change if you do not begin with a firm commitment to at least investigate your mind to see what you find and to see if there is another way of being in the world. This time is your time, and the results of spending the time working with your mind are your results. While the results may benefit others, ultimately the benefit is yours. So committing the time to really learn how to work with your mind is a positive way of being "selfish." It's a way to deepen your relationship with yourself and to become more present with your life, which is precious.

Appendix B: Practice Schedule

The schedule that follows is an example that you can use to set aside the time necessary to learn some of the techniques and methods found within this book and to listen to the guided practices from the CD, MP3s, or downloads that I've provided. While it's not necessary to follow these examples precisely, some approximation of this kind of routine and discipline will definitely assist you in progressing rapidly in your practice. Most of all, be flexible and open with your schedule. If you find that there are days when you can spend more time or wish to spend more time with the practices, go for it! And if there are days when you're simply too busy to meet a precise time schedule, then have the space and flexibility to alter your practice, maybe cutting it up into smaller but more frequent periods. Finally, have fun! It's your mind; enjoy it.

WEEK	A.M.	P.M.	EXERCISE	COMMENTS
1	5 Minutes	10 Minutes	Track #1: "Riding the Breath"	Have fun; this is just the beginning.
2	10 Minutes	10 Minutes	Track #1: "Riding the Breath" and/or Track #2: "Beginning with Your Thoughts"	Same as last week: have fun; this is just the beginning.
3	10 Minutes	15 Minutes	Track #1: "Riding the Breath" and/or Track #2: "Beginning With Your Thoughts"	In fact, no matter where you are in the process, have fun!
4	15 Minutes	15 Minutes	Track #1: "Riding the Breath" and/or Track #2: "Beginning With Your Thoughts" Track #3: "Caring for a Loved One"	If you're keeping up with this, then you're practicing 30 minutes a day!
5	15 Minutes	20 Minutes	Track #1: "Riding the Breath" and/or Track #2: "Beginning With Your Thoughts" Track #4: "Loving-Kindness Practice"	Use whatever tracks work for you; the exercise suggestions are just to keep you focused.

WEEK	A.M.	P.M.	EXERCISE	COMMENTS
6	20 Minutes	20 Minutes	Track #1: "Riding the Breath" Track #5: "Working with Our Thoughts"	Try to use these two exercises each day this week.
7	20 Minutes	25 Minutes	Track #1: "Riding the Breath" Track #6: "Mindfulness, Awareness, and Spaciousness in Meditation"	You're now practicing 45 minutes a day; way to go! That's what we should strive for.
8	30 Minutes in the morning or..	30 Minutes at night or in the evening.	Track #6: "Mindfulness, Awareness, and Spaciousness in Meditation" Track # 7: "Training in a Compassionate Impulse"	At this point, if you can't practice twice a day for 30 minutes, do it either in the morning or at night.
9	35 Minutes in the morning or…	35 Minutes at night or in the evening.	Track #1: "Riding the Breath" Track # 8: "Working with Difficult Thoughts and Emotions"	Unless you wish to do two long sessions a day, choose morning or night.
10	40 Minutes in the morning or…	40 Minutes at night or in the evening.	Track # 8: "Working with Difficult Thoughts and Emotions" Track # 9: "Tonglen"	Unless you wish to do two long sessions a day, choose morning or night.
11	45 Minutes in the morning or…	45 Minutes at night on in the evening.	Use any track or none at all. Ultimately, you'll want to rely on the presence of your mind and nothing else.	Unless you wish to do two long sessions a day, choose morning or night.
12	45 Minutes in the morning or…	45 Minutes at night or in the evening.	Use any track or none at all. Ultimately, you'll want to rely on the presence of your mind and nothing else.	Unless you wish to do two long sessions a day, choose morning or night.

Appendix C: Daily Activities and Opportunities for Practice

Life is immensely rich with many things, but one thing that we don't usually view our lives being rich in is time. Especially if we live a busy and active life, the last thing that we seem to have enough of is time. And when it comes to taking on any new projects or learning new things, the time may seem to diminish even more. So how can we take what we learn in our structured or "formal" practice and put it into practice in our daily life?

There's a Zen saying, "Chop wood, carry water." What this means is that when one chops wood, one remains mindful, attentive, and aware of the fact that one is chopping wood. And when one carries water, one remains mindful, attentive, and aware that one is carrying water. Seems simple. The problem is that not many of us chop wood or carry water on a regular basis, unless the water is in a basin for a bed-bath or in a pot for making pasta.

My son, Noah, and I have modified the saying a bit to work with our modern lives. Bear in mind that as of the writing of this book, Noah is only five and a half. Still, he understands the conversations around being mindful and aware, and so he says, "Brush teeth, play soccer!" It seems to work; when we're brushing teeth, we work really hard on not becoming distracted while doing so. Actually, what is amazing is that when I share this idea with most adults, they tell me that they oftentimes don't even remember the act of brushing their teeth; they just do it automatically. Exactly!! It's the automaticity of our daily lives from which we're trying to awaken, so that when we do anything—like brush our teeth—we're present and aware. Granted, brushing one's teeth may not seem like a particularly important event to be engaged in, but that's not really the point. The point is that if we can become engaged enough in all of the menial acts that we do during the day—driving, brushing teeth, staring at a computer screen, taking a shower—then all of our "activities of daily living" can become moments of practice.

Think about it; if you drive anywhere—to work, to go shopping, to pick up children— you've got the perfect place and time to take the practice off the cushion (referring to the cushion that some people choose to meditate upon) and out into the world. And, after all, we're not trying to learn these techniques so that we can sit in a chair or on a cushion and become more mindful, aware, and compassionate; we're working with our mind to be more present in the world.

So, here's a very short list of some times when you can practice in your daily life. It is by no means complete or by any means exhaustive; it's just a beginning.

1. While taking a shower
2. While brushing your teeth
3. While eating
4. While eating...did I say this twice? Right, how many of us rush through our meals without even remembering what it was that we ate? Eating is *one of the best times* to practice being mindful and aware. It's amazing how our food intake, what we take into our body, how much we eat, and—surprise!—how much we gain weight can be due to not being present with what we're eating. Try it! You have three times a day to work with this one.
5. While driving to: work, school, play, shop, run errands, vacations, distraction.
6. While surfing the web or being otherwise involved on the computer. Who knows, you may be less inclined to impulse-buy on the Internet.
7. While exercising. This is a great one. I used to run a lot—marathons, 10k, etc. I also still like to bicycle quite a bit. But how to find the time to practice when I want to bike? Exactly; practice while biking. This means seeing my surroundings, feeling the road, smelling the smells, feeling my heart pounding, noticing the patterns of my breathing. Zen and the art of biking!
8. While at work. Right, this *is* why we're learning about this, isn't it? What about when you're taking care of someone who is being difficult? Or who's dying? Or who's unconscious on a ventilator? Or who's giving birth? What about when your boss is telling you that you need to work harder? Or less hard? Or maybe you're the boss? Right. Work.
9. Stuck at a traffic light? Meditate. But don't forget to be aware of the light. This isn't about spacing out, remember? *Gee; what are those cars behind me honking at me for? I'm at one with the light...except that it's green!*
10. Folding laundry.
11. Doing the dishes. I love this one. As a kid, my mom figured out early on that kids were valuable...for doing the dishes. I think that I became a Zen dishwasher at the age of 10!
12. When you're sick.
13. When you're in pain.
14. When you're sad or when you're happy.
15. And the list goes on and on. Truly, since we're trying to become more present and less distracted at any and all moments, there's never a time where practicing won't work. Try it.

Resources:

There are quite literally thousands of books, centers, teachers, and methods that you can use to train in a variety of mindfulness, meditative, and compassion techniques. It is not my intention to present a complete list but to give you a few leads in the direction that may best suit you. Many of the websites that I list will have links that will send you to other websites, ad nauseam. Don't get overwhelmed, take your time, find something that calls to you.

To make all of the books that I list accessible to you, I have set up a "bookstore" on my website where you can link to a variety of sites to purchase the books. That doesn't mean that you have to purchase any of them or that you have to use my website. They're simply there for your use if you choose to use them.

By providing links to sites, I am not endorsing any or all of them. Think of this more as a directory than as a guide. Your discernment and personal preference will ultimately determine what you choose to use and what you choose not to use.

If you are interested in finding a teacher, mentor, or instructor, I encourage you to find someone with whom you feel a personal connection. The teachers that I list here are those who I know something about, have studied with, or who my acquaintances have studied with.

Suggested Readings and Materials:

Here is a list of books, many of which may help you to deepen your understanding of meditation, different methods of mindfulness and its relationship to your health and everyday life. I've tried to round out this list with material from different traditions and perspectives. You may find that reading books from a variety of sources helps you to gain a wider view of the many aspects of working with the mind. Or you may wish to focus on one path or tradition.

Within this list are a number of texts whose words I've cited in this book. If any of the citations that I used were of interest to you, I encourage you to explore their sources and see if there are additional passages that inspire you.

While I have read many of the books on this list and found them to be of great value in deepening the foundation of my understanding of meditation, it has been through the practical application of this book knowledge that I've found real stability within my practice. And so, please remember that only by practicing these methods can you realize their greatest benefits. These books are to support you in your practice but should not be used as a substitute for it. Use these materials as inspiration, reading them at times when you are not practicing, between sessions, or during session breaks. Perhaps reading a few pages will be all that you need to inspire you to spend the time that you need to deepen your understanding of and relationship with your mind. Enjoy!

Bodian, Stephan. *Meditation for Dummies*. New York NY: Wiley Publishing Inc., 1999.

Boorstein, Sylvia. *It's Easier Than You Think*. San Francisco: HarperOne, 1997.

Chodron, Pema. *Start Where You Are*. Boston: Shambhala, 1994.*The Wisdom of No Escape*. Shambhala, 2010.
- *When Things Fall Apart*. Shambhala, 2000.

Cowan, John. *Taking Jesus Seriously: Buddhist Meditation for Christians*. Collegeville: Liturgical Press, 2004

Davis, Avram. *Meditation from the Heart of Judaism.* Woodstock: Jewish Lights Publishing, 1997.

Finley, James. *Christian Meditation: Experiencing the Presence of God.* New York: HarperCollins, 2004.

Goldstein, Joseph. *Insight Meditation—The Practice of Freedom.* Boston: Shambhala, 1993.

Goleman, Daniel. *The Meditative Mind: The Varieties of Meditative Experience.* New York: Jeremy P. Tarcher/Putnam, 1988.

Hanh, Thich Nhat. *Happiness: Essential Mindfulness Practices.* Berkeley; Parallax Press, 2009.

   - *Taming the Tiger Within: Meditations on Transforming Difficult Emotions.* New York: Penguin Group. 2005.

Hanh, Thich Nhat and Lilian Cheung. *Savor: Mindful Eating, Mindful Life.* New York: HarperOne, 2010.

Hanh, Thich Nhat, Arnold Kotler, and H. H. the Dalai Lama. *Peace Is Every Step: The Path of Mindfulness in Everyday Life.* New York: Bantam Books, 1992.

Hanh, Thich Nhat, Vo-Dihn Mai, and Mobi Ho. *The Miracle of Mindfulness.* Boston: Beacon Press, 1979.

Hanh, Thich Nhat, Melvin McLeod, and Sherab Chodzin Kohn. *You Are Here: Discovering the Magic of the Present Moment.* Boston: Shambhala, 2009.

Jackson, Phil. *Sacred Hoops: Spiritual Lessons of a Hardwood Warrior.* New York: Hyperion, 1995.

Johnston, William. *Christian Zen.* New York: Fordham University Press, 1997.

Kabat-Zinn, Jon. *Coming to Our Senses: Healing Ourselves and the World Through Mindfulness.* New York: Hyperion, 2005.

   - *Full Catastrophe Living: Using the Wisdom of Your Body and Mind to Face Stress, Pain and Illness.* New York: Dell Publishing, 1990.

   - *Wherever You Go, There You Are: Mindfulness Meditation in Everyday Life.* New York: Hyperion, 2004.

Kabat-Zinn, Jon and Myla.. *Everyday Blessings: A Guide to Mindful Parenting.* New York: Hyperion, 1997.

Kabatznick, Ronna. *The Zen of Eating.* New York: Berkeley Publishing Group, 1998.

Kaplan, Aryeh. *Jewish Meditation: A Practical Guide.* New York: Schoken Books, 1985.

Kornfield, Jack. *A Path with Heart: A Guide Through the Perils and*

Promises of Spiritual Life. New York: Bantam Books, 1993.

Rabinowitz, Ilana. *Mountains are Mountains and Rivers are Rivers: Applying Eastern Teachings to Everyday Life*. New York: Hyperion, 1999.

Rinpoche, Chokyi Nyima with David R. Shlim, MD. *Medicine and Compassion: A Tibetan Lama's Guidance for Caregivers*. Somerville: Wisdom Publications, 2004.

Rinpoche, Yongey Mingyur. *The Joy of Living: Unlocking the Secret and Science of Happiness.* New York: Three Rivers Press, 2007.

Rinpoche, Sogyal. *The Tibetan Book of Living and Dying*. New York: HarperCollins, 2002.

Rinpoche, Tulku Thondrup. *The Healing Power of Mind: Simple Meditation Exercises for Health, Well-Being, and Enlightenment*. Boston: Shambhala, 1996.

Santorelli, Sake. *Heal Thy Self: Lessons on Mindfulness in Medicine*. New York: Bell Tower. 2000.

Sapolsky, Robert. *Why Zebras Don't Get Ulcers*. New York: Henry Holt and Company, LLC., 2004.

Segal, Zindel V., Mark G. Williams and John D. Teasdale. *Mindfulness-Based Cognitive Therapy for Depression: A New Approach to Preventing Relapse*. New York: The Guilford Press, 2002.

Sobel, David S., Robert Ornstein. *The Healthy Mind, Healthy Body Handbook*. Los Altos: DRX, 1996.

Tulku, Tarthang. *Gesture of Balance: A Guide to Awareness, Self-Healing, and Meditation*. Berkeley: Dharma Publishing, 1977.

Vieten, Cassandra. *Mindful Motherhood: Practical Tools for Staying Sane During Pregnancy and Your Child's First Year*. Oakland: New Harbinger Press, 2009.

Suggested Centers for Learning Mindfulness and Meditation:

There are literally thousands of centers and places to go to learn a variety of mindfulness and meditation techniques. First off I would suggest that you investigate any center carefully, making sure that you read through its website and any publications associated with it. There may be many centers, but there might be only one or two, or a handful, that offer what you particularly need. Use discernment, mindfulness, and awareness when considering any location for studying these practices.

While I can't attest to the level of training or to the expertise of guidance that you'll receive at any centers where I haven't personally trained, I am familiar enough with the following centers to suggest them as potential starting points on your path. Again, it will be up to you to make sure that the fit is right. Should you investigate any one of these centers and find that they do not teach what they purport to teach, or simply aren't centers of excellence, or should you find that they are no longer in existence, please do contact me and send me feedback.

In reviewing these sites, even if a particular tradition isn't the basis of your belief, I encourage you to investigate its programs anyway, at least reading about its programs and courses on its website. For instance, I would suggest that you not shy away from programs that have some reference to Buddhist approaches since this is the discipline that brought the practices of "mindfulness" to the West. In fact, many great Christian meditation programs have been inspired by teachers of Buddhism. And, likewise, many of the Western teachers of Buddhism were raised within the Judeo-Christian traditions.

UNAFFILIATED CENTERS:

* If you do an internet search for "mindfulness meditation program," you will find a number of centers with mindfulness as their basis. I encourage you to explore those programs affiliated with a medical-center, or ones that have a

track-record of ongoing classes and retreats. While some of the programs that you find may have an affiliation with Buddhism, there are quite a few with an ecumenical approach.

The Center for Mindfulness in Medicine, Healthcare, and Society
Website: http://www.umassmed.edu/cfm/home/index.aspx
The Center for Mindfulness is an innovative leader in mind-body medicine and mindfulness-based treatment and research investigations, pioneering the integration of meditation and mindfulness into mainstream medicine and health care. Located at the University of Massachusetts and established in 1995 by Dr. Jon Kabat-Zinn, the Center is an out-growth of the acclaimed Stress Reduction Clinic, the oldest and largest academic medical center –based stress reduction program in the world.

CHRISTIAN MEDITATION PROGRAMS:
The Center For Action And Contemplation
Website: http://cacradicalgrace.org
The Center for Action and Contemplation, located in Albuquerque, New Mexico, was founded in 1987 by Franciscan Father Richard Rohr, who saw the need for a training/formation center. It serves as a place of discernment and growth for activists and those interested in social service ministries-a place to be still, and learn how to integrate a contemplative lifestyle with compassionate service. The Center's purpose is to serve not only as a forum for peaceful, non-violent social change but also as a radical voice for renewal and encouragement.

Contemplative Outreach
Website: http://www.contemplativeoutreach.org
Contemplative Outreach is a spiritual network of individuals and small faith communities committed to living the contemplative dimension of the Gospel. The common desire for Divine transformation, primarily expressed through a commitment to a daily Centering Prayer practice, unites this international, interdenominational community. Contemplative Outreach annually serves over 40,000 people; supports over 120 active contemplative chapters in 39 countries; supports over 800 prayer groups; teaches over 15,000 people the practice of Centering Prayer and other contemplative practices through locally-hosted workshops; and provides training and resources to local chapters and volunteers.

The Contemplative Society

Website: http://www.contemplative.org

The Contemplative Society is an inclusive non-profit association that encourages a deepening of contemplative prayer based in the Christian tradition while also welcoming and being supportive of other meditation traditions. It offers a consistent and balanced path for spiritual growth and transformation rooted in prayer, silence, mindful work, and in the 1500-year-old wisdom of our Benedictine contemplative heritage.

The Contemplative Spirituality Network

Website: http://www.contemplativespirituality.org/about.html

Located in Victoria, British Columbia, The Contemplative Spirituality Network seeks to offer support for an interior journey of transformation within the Christian contemplative tradition through encouraging contemplative prayer in daily life, giving rise to social action and justice, and promoting the study, and relevance of the Christian mystical tradition in the contemporary world.

The Contemplative Way

Website: http://www.contemplativeway.org

James Finley, Ph.D. lived as a monk at the cloistered Trappist monastery of the Abbey of Gethsemani in Kentucky, where the world-renowned monk and author, Thomas Merton, was his spiritual director. James Finley leads retreats and workshops throughout the United States and Canada, attracting men and women from all religious traditions who seek to live a contemplative way of life in the midst of today's busy world. He is also a clinical psychologist in private practice with his wife in Santa Monica, California.

Oasis Of Wisdom

Website: http://www.oasisofwisdom.net

The Oasis of Wisdom is a center offering resources, retreats and guidance for people who live busy and responsible lives. The center's path is rooted in the life and wisdom of Jesus, the Christ, yet it honors and is richly influenced by other religious traditions. Retreats are held at the center and at sites throughout the United States.

Pacific Center For Spiritual Formation

Website: http://www.pcentersf.org

Since its beginnings in 1984, the Pacific Center for Spiritual Formation [PCSF] has sought to offer opportunities for individuals, groups, and congregations to experience a deeper awareness of God. Rooted in the Christian contemplative tradition, ecumenical in composition, and committed to interfaith practice, PCSF is a resource for contemplative enrichment in the San Francisco Bay area.

Pendle Hill
Website: http://www.pendlehill.org
Pendle Hill is a Quaker center for spiritual growth, study and service. At Pendle Hill, students and staff live, work, worship and study together. Located on 23 wooded acres just outside of Philadelphia, PA, Pendle Hill is where adults and youth come for inspiration and renewal. Founded by Quakers in 1930, Pendle Hill is a community that welcomes people from many faiths and countries.

The World Community for Christian Meditation
www.wccm.org
In 2011 this community celebrates its twentieth birthday. Our roots lie in the life and teaching of the Benedictine monk John Main and in the western monastic wisdom that formed him. The roots in the tradition feed the branches of the community that have spread to bring the benefits of this simple practice to many – of all backgrounds and stages of life. The community emphasizes a regular twice-daily practice of meditation. The simplicity of this discipline is its contribution to the needs of our time.

Founded in 1991 The World Community for Christian Meditation is now present in 114 countries. More than 2000 weekly groups meet in churches, schools universities, offices, prisons and hospitals – the tip of an iceberg of a grass-roots community of individual meditators. Sixteen Christian Meditation Centres, from Jakarta to Los Angeles, also share the teaching through retreats and seminars.

JEWISH MEDITATION PROGRAMS:
The Awakened Heart Project for Contemplative Judaism
http://www.awakenedheartproject.org
The mission of Awakened Heart Project is to promote the use of Jewish contemplative techniques that foster the development of a heart of wisdom and compassion. Cultivating an awakened heart leads to acting in the world with

loving-kindness towards all beings recognizing them as manifestations of the Holy One of Being. The AHP provides opportunities for a focused effort at refining contemplative Jewish practices, such as meditation and prayer, as well as creating opportunities for intensive practice. Courses and retreats are held in the United States and abroad.

Chochmat HaLev

http://www.chochmat.org

A Jewish retreat and meditation center in the San Francisco Bay Area, Chochmat HaLev offers Jewish healing conferences, chant retreats, Jewish meditation sitting groups, and more.

The Elat Chayyim Center for Jewish Spirituality

http://isabellafreedman.org/jewish-retreats/elatchayyim

The Elat Chayyim Center for Jewish Spirituality continues to offer the transformational and cutting-edge retreat experiences carried over from Elat Chayyim in Accord, NY. Its year-round programs promote practices that draw on the wisdom of Jewish tradition and reflect the values and consciousness of our evolving society. Experiential approaches to Jewish learning, ritual and prayer are designed to help retreatants on their search to cultivate awareness of the Divine presence in all aspects of life.

ISLAM/SUFI MEDITATION PROGRAMS:

Dervish Retreat Center

http://www.whirlingdervish.org

The Dervish Retreat Center is a 60-acre facility located in Spencer, New York, founded by Sheikha Khadija Radin in 1999. It offers events and studies in Sufi and other cultural and mystical traditions. There are classes that offer Mevlevi whirling, as well as other forms of whirling, zikr breath, hand drumming, meditation, Eastern, and Middle Eastern philosophies. It also offers personal retreats in early spring. Participants are encouraged to experience for themselves activities that facilitate concentration, awareness and total absorption into practices which promote a centered and present state. Each person works at his/her own level and pace. There is a warm, supportive, and relaxed atmosphere amongst the community members. All religious affiliations, races, and cultures are welcome and respected.

Sufi Order Retreats

http://sufiorderretreats.net

This site provides referrals to places for individuals to rest and restore themselves, to turn within and rediscover their source, and to know the deep stillness that is the wellspring of authentic guidance. Individuals are encouraged to leave behind thoughts and concerns of everyday life in order to "go within" to discover a deeper self and the fundamental inter-connectedness with all dimensions of being. This way of being gives an opportunity to recognize qualities in oneself not always perceived in everyday life and affords a new vantage point from which to view one's life and problems. Finally, consciously integrating these insights into the fabric of one's personality, one is prepared to re-enter active life, with a renewed vision of identity and purpose.

BUDDHIST MEDITATION PROGRAMS:

* If you do an internet search for "Buddhist meditation," you will find thousands of sites and links. While there are countless teachers of meditation, based upon the Buddhist contemplative traditions, I encourage you to fully explore these sites, what they have to offer, and most importantly, the teachers who are offering the courses.

Deer Park Monastery

http://www.deerparkmonastery.org

Deer Park Monastery is a community in the tradition of Thich Nhat Hanh and the Plum Village Practice Center. This 400-acre sanctuary rests peacefully in the chaparral mountains of southern California, surrounded and protected by oaks and the natural landscape. It was established in July 2000 by the Plum Village Community. Now, it is a safe and serene refuge for many practitioners to come and learn the art of mindful living and practicing with a community.

Mindfulness Practice Center of Fairfax

http://www.mpcf.org

Based on Zen practices and the teachings of Thich Nhat Hanh, The Mindfulness Practice Center of Fairfax offers sessions of training in and practice of mindfulness in a non-sectarian way. Sessions are offered in the secluded setting of the Unitarian Universalist Congregation in Oakton, Virginia. It is a quiet, beautiful and spiritual space.

Plum Village

http://www.plumvillage.org/

One of the best known and most respected Zen masters in the world today, poet, and peace and human rights activist, Thich Nhat Hanh has led an extraordinary life. His life long efforts to generate peace and reconciliation moved Martin Luther King, Jr. to nominate him for the Nobel Peace Prize in 1967. He founded the Van Hanh Buddhist University in Saigon and the School for Youths of Social Services in Vietnam. When not travelling the world to teach "The Art of Mindful Living", he teaches, writes, and gardens in Plum Village, France, a Buddhist monastery for monks and nuns and a mindfulness practice center for lay people. He has received recognition for his work with Vietnam veterans, meditation retreats, and his prolific writings on meditation, mindfulness, and peace. He has published some 85 titles of accessible poems, prose, and prayers, with more than 40 in English, including the best selling *Call Me by My True Names*, *Peace Is Every Step*, *Being Peace*, *Touching Peace*, and *Living Buddha Living Christ*. In September of 2003 he addressed members of the US Congress, leading them through a two-day retreat.

Pundarika Foundation

http://www.pundarika.org/

For over 15 years, Tsoknyi Rinpoche has been teaching students worldwide about the innermost nature of mind in the Tibetan Buddhist tradition. Rinpoche is one of those rare teachers whose lighthearted, yet illuminating style appeals to both beginners and advanced practitioners alike. He is truly a bridge between ancient wisdom and the modern mind. His fresh insights into the western psyche have enabled him to teach and write in a way that touches our most profound awareness, using metaphors, stories and images that point directly to our everyday experience. He is widely recognized as a brilliant meditation teacher, is the author of two books, Carefree Dignity and Fearless Simplicity, and has a keen interest in the ongoing dialogue between western research, especially in neuroscience, and Buddhist practitioners and scholars

Rigpa

http://usa.rigpa.org/

Founded by Sogyal Rinpoche, author of *The Tibetan Book of Living and Dying*, Rigpa aims to present the Buddhist tradition of Tibet in a way that is both completely authentic, and as relevant as possible to the lives and needs of modern men and women. Open to all schools and traditions of Buddhist wisdom, and with the guidance and gracious patronage of His Holiness the Dalai Lama, Rigpa offers those following the Buddhist teachings a complete path of study and practice, along with the environment they need to experience the teachings fully. *The Tibetan Book of Living and Dying* has sold over 1.6 million copies, in 27 languages and 54 countries. It has been adopted by colleges, groups and institutions, both medical and religious, and is used extensively by nurses, doctors and health care professionals. Rigpa has more than 130 centers in 41 countries all over the world. For people who do not live close to a center, Rigpa offers a full curriculum of courses in Buddhism, meditation and compassion online. Rigpa also has three retreat centers dedicated to providing secluded and inspiring environments in which people can study and practice the Buddhist teachings.

Spirit Rock
http://www.spiritrock.org/
Located just north of San Francisco, Spirit Rock Meditation Center is dedicated to the teachings of the Buddha as presented in the vipassana tradition. The practice of mindful awareness, called Insight or Vipassana Meditation, is at the heart of all the activities at Spirit Rock. The Center hosts a full program of ongoing classes, daylong programs, and residential retreats.

Shambhala
http://www.shambhala.org/
It is the Shambhala view that every human being has a fundamental nature of goodness, warmth and intelligence. This nature can be cultivated through meditation, following ancient principles, and it can be further developed in daily life, so that it radiates out to family, friends, community and society. Shambhala's vision is rooted in the contemplative teachings of Buddhism, yet is a fresh expression of the spiritual journey for our time; it is available to practitioners of any tradition. Shambhala draws on the wisdom of the Kagyu and Nyingma schools of Tibetan Buddhism as inherited by founder of Shambhala, Chögyam Trungpa, and his son and spiritual heir, Sakyong Mipham. With centers located throughout the world, this tradition teaches how to live in the secular world with courage and compassion.

Tergar
http://tergar.org
The mission of the Tergar Meditation Community is to make the ancient practice of meditation accessible to the modern world. For centuries, the prac-

tice of meditation has been used by countless individuals to transform suffering into joy and confusion into wisdom. Tergar meditation and study programs are designed to facilitate this transformation. Under the guidance of Yongey Mingyur Rinpoche, a remarkable teacher celebrated for his ability to make the practice of meditation accessible to people of all backgrounds, the Tergar community of meditation centers and practice groups, located worldwide, provides a comprehensive course of meditation training and study, with programs for Buddhists and non-Buddhists alike.

Vipassana Meditation Centers

http://www.dhamma.org

Vipassana, which means to see things as they really are, is one of Indiaís most ancient techniques of meditation. It was taught in India more than 2500 years ago as a universal remedy for universal ills. The technique of Vipassana Meditation is taught at ten-day residential courses during which participants learn the basics of the method, and practice sufficiently to experience its beneficial results. There are no charges for the courses - not even to cover the cost of food and accommodation. All expenses are met by donations from people who, having completed a course and experienced the benefits of Vipassana, wish to give others the opportunity to also benefit. Courses are given in numerous Meditation Centers and at non-center course locations at rented sites. Each location has its own schedule of courses. There are numerous Centers in India and elsewhere in Asia/Pacific; ten Centers in North America; three Centers in Latin America; eight Centers in Europe; seven Centers in Australia/New Zealand; one Center in the Middle East and one Center in Africa.

Sources

.

1   Joe, GW, Simpson, DD, Dansereau, DF, Rowan-Szal, GA.
"Relationships between Counseling Rapport and Drug Abuse Treatment Outcomes." *Psychiatric Services,* 2001 Sep;52(9):1223-9.

OBJECTIVE: This study examined the association between counseling rapport and drug-abuse treatment outcomes.

METHODS: Two cohorts of outpatients who were being treated with methadone in four cities were studied. In this study, 354 patients comprised Cohort 1 in community-based nonprofit programs, and 223 patients from a private for-profit program comprised Cohort 2. Logistic-regression analyses were used to assess the importance of counseling rapport as a predictor of drug use and criminality relative to treatment retention in the index treatment, satisfaction with treatment, and whether additional treatment was received after the index treatment.

RESULTS: In both cohorts, ratings made by counselors, during treatment, of therapeutic involvement and relationships with patients provided a useful measure of counseling rapport. A lower level of rapport during treatment predicted worse postindex treatment outcomes, including more cocaine use and criminality, both by itself and after adjustment for treatment retention, satisfaction with treatment, and postindex treatment status. Counseling strategies were associated with the development of counseling rapport.

CONCLUSIONS: Counseling rapport is a vital part of the therapeutic process and helps explain why and when treatment is effective. It contributes explicitly to the prediction of outcomes, apart from treatment retention, and accounts in part for the usual association between treatment retention and outcomes.

2   Gilbert, DA, Hayes, E. "Communication and Outcomes of Visits Between Older Patients and Nurse Practitioners." *Nursing Research,* 2009 Jul-Aug;58(4):283-93.

BACKGROUND: Effective patient-clinician communication is at the heart of good health care and may be even more vital for older patients and their nurse practitioners (NPs).

OBJECTIVES: To examine contributions of older patients' and NPs' characteristics and the content and relationship components of their communication to patients' proximal outcomes (satisfaction and intention to adhere) and longer-term outcomes (changes in presenting problems, physical health, and mental health), and contributions of proximal outcomes to longer-term outcomes.

METHODS: Visits of a statewide sample of 31 NPs and 155 older patients were video-recorded. Patients' and NPs' communication during visits was measured using the Roter Interaction Analysis System for verbal activities, a check sheet for nonverbal activities, and an inventory of relationship-dimension items. Proximal outcomes were measured with single items after visits. At four weeks, change in presenting problems was measured with a single item, and physical and mental-health changes were measured with the SF-12v2 Health Survey. Mixed-model regression with backward deletion was conducted until only predictors with $p \leq .05$ remained in the models.

RESULTS: With the other variables in the models held constant, better outcomes were related to background characteristics of poorer baseline health, unmanaged care settings, and more NP experience; to a content component of seeking and giving biomedical and psychosocial information; and to a relationship component of more positive talk and greater trust and receptivity and affection, depth, and similarity. Poorer outcomes were associated with higher rates of lifestyle discussion and NPs' rapport-building that patients may have perceived to be patronizing. Greater intention to adhere was associated with greater improvement in presenting problems.

DISCUSSION: Older patient–NP communication was effective regarding seeking and giving biomedical and psychosocial information other than that involving lifestyle. Studies of ways to improve older patient–NP lifestyle discussions and rapport-building are needed.

3   Rinpoche, Chokyi Nyima, Shlim, David R. *Medicine and Compassion—A Tibetan Lama's Guidance for Caregivers*. Boston: Wisdom Publications, 2004, pg. 33–34.

4   This quote, attributed to the late Joseph Campbell, is a common way that individuals across many spiritual disciplines view the daily human experience. That is, to participate fully in the world knowing that much of what one does can change at any moment and can even lead to suffering or sorrow.

5   Rinpoche, Sogyal. *The Tibetan Book of Living and Dying.* San Francisco: Harper, 1992, pg. 187.

6   Schuman, Marjorie. *The Psychobiology of Consciousness*, eds. J. Davidson and R. Davidson. New York: Plenum Press, 1980, pgs. 333–378.

7   Rinpoche, Sogyal. *The Tibetan Book of Living and Dying.* San Francisco: Harper Collins, 2002, pgs. 58–59.

8   Austin, James. *Zen and the Brain.* Boston; MIT Press, 2000, pgs. 93–99. For a brilliant discussion on the uses of the breath within meditation, as well as some of the complex physiology behind the meditative breath, author James Austin, MD, enters into the discussion in Chapter 22 of his in-depth book *Zen and the Brain.* I highly recommend this book for anyone interested in reading an exhaustive investigation into meditation, particularly Zen meditation, by the former professor emeritus of Neurology at the University of Colorado Health Sciences Center.

9   Rinpoche, Sogyal. *The Tibetan Book of Living and Dying.* San Francisco: Harper Collins, 2002. pg. 60.

10   Rinpoche, Yongey Mingyur. *The Joy of Living: Unlocking the Secret and Science of Happiness.* New York: Three Rivers Press, 2007, pg. 140.

11   Amati M, Tomasetti M, Ciuccarelli M, Mariotti L, Tarquini LM, Bracci M, Baldassari M, Balducci C, Alleva R, Borghi B, Mocchegiani E, Copertaro A, Santarelli L. "Relationship of Job Satisfaction, Psychological Distress and Stress-Related Biological Parameters Among Healthy Nurses: A Longitudinal Study." *Journal of Occupational Health*, 201:52(1):31–8.

OBJECTIVE: To examine the relationship between job satisfaction, psychological distress, psychosocial processes, and stress-related biological factors and to evaluate whether, over time, changes of work satisfaction could affect the immunological-inflammatory status of workers.

METHODS: One-hundred-one nurses were enrolled at the Clinic of Occupational Medicine, Polytechnic University of Marche, Ancona, Italy. Perceived job satisfaction, psychological distress, and social support were assessed every four months over a one-year period using four self-reported questionnaires. T lymphocytes CD3, CD4(+), CD8(+), CD8(+)-CD57(+), B lymphocyte CD19(+), NK cells CD56(+), and NK cell activity were determined.

RESULTS: Job satisfaction was associated with reduced psychological distress and was characterized by low cell numbers of CD8(+) suppressor T cells, CD8(+)-CD57(+) activated T cells, CD56(+) NK cells and low IL-6 levels. Over time, changes in psychological parameters were related to changes in the immunological-inflammatory variables. Subjects who increased their job satisfaction showed a reduced psychological stress associated with reduced number of CD8(+)-CD57(+) activated T cells and inflammatory cytokines.

CONCLUSIONS: Job (dis)satisfaction is related with psychological mechanisms in stress affecting cellular immune function.

12   This quote, from the book *Zen and the Brain*, by the author James H. Austin, MD, begins a discussion on the "topography" of awareness. I'll tout Austin's book many times throughout my book; it's sensational! If you want a very thorough understanding of the brain in its relation to meditative practices and a deeper insight into a Zen practitioner's experience of the neuroscience of meditation, this is the book! *Zen and the Brain*. Cambridge, MA: MIT Press, 2000, pg. 296.

13   Kabat-Zinn, Jon. *Coming to Our Senses*. New York: Hyperion, 2005, pgs. 405–406.

14   Rinpoche, Sogyal. *The Tibetan Book of Living and Dying*. San Francisco: Harper Collins, 2002, pg. 77.

15   Finley, James. *Christian Meditation*. San Francisco: Harper, 2004, pg. 279.

16   Lerner, Michael. Jewish Renewal: A Path to Healing and Transformation. New York: HarperCollins, 1994, pgs. 112-113.

17   Lerner, Michael. Jewish Renewal: A Path to Healing and Transformation. New York: HarperCollins, 1994, pg. 206.

18   Dalai Lama. *Ethics for the New Millennium*. New York: Riverhead Books, 1999, pg. 123.

19   Letter of 1950, as quoted in the *New York Times* (29 March 1972) and the *New York Post* (28 November 1972). However, *The New Quotable Einstein* by Alice Calaprice (Princeton University Press, 2005: ISBN 0691120749), p. 206, has a different and presumably more accurate version of this letter, which she dates to February 12, 1950, and describes as "a letter to a distraught father who had lost his young son and had asked Einstein for some comforting words." The actual quote is presented as "A human being is a part of the whole, called by us "Universe," a part limited in time and space. He experiences himself, his thoughts and feelings as something separate from the rest—a kind of optical delusion of his consciousness. The striving to free oneself from this delusion is the one issue of true religion. Not to nourish it but to try to overcome it is the way to reach the attainable measure of piece of mind."

20   Austin, James H. *Zen and the Brain*. Cambridge: MIT Press, 2000, pg. 651.

21   Shlim, David R. and Rinpoche, Chokyi Nyima. *Medicine and Com-*

passion—A Tibetan Lama's Guidance for Caregivers. Boston: Wisdom Publications, 2004, pg. 3. This quote reminds us of what has often been referred to as "high touch." As opposed to high tech, high touch involves a high degree of personal contact that is based on compassion and presence and not just on our technology, however truly amazing it may be.

22   Wicks, Robert. *Living a Gentle, Passionate Life.* Mahwah, NJ: Paulist Press, 1998, pgs. 29–30.

23   Shlim, David R. and Rinpoche, Chokyi Nyima. *Medicine and Compassion—A Tibetan Lama's Guidance for Caregivers.* Boston: Wisdom Publications, 2004, pg. 71.

24   Merton, Thomas. *A Vow of Conversation: Journals 1964–1965.* Ed. Naomi Burton Stone. New York: Farrar, Straus and Giroux, 1999, pg. 161.

25   This is the paraphrase of a statement that the late Tibetan master, Dudjom Rinpoche, used to teach with. It is based on the notion that our sense faculties are able to "merely" perceive without our mind needing to become involved in the perceiving. This way, we can leave all that we perceive within the realm of the sense faculty that perceives it, without becoming emotionally involved in the object. We begin to do this by gaining some "space" between our thoughts about something and our reaction to our thoughts. And we open up this space through the practice of mindfulness and awareness.

26   Goldstein, Joseph. *Insight Meditation.* Boston: Shambala, 1994, pgs. 59–60.

27   Austin, James H. *Zen and the Brain.* Cambridge: MIT Press, 2000, pg. 127.

28   Goldstein, Joseph. *Insight Meditation.* Boston: Shambala, 1994, pgs. 59–60.

29   Kabat-Zinn, Jon. *Coming to Our Senses.* New York: Hyperion, 2005, pgs. 88–89.

30   Finley, James. *Christian Meditation.* San Francisco: Harper, 2004, pg. 279.

31   Rinpoche, Sogyal. *Glimpse After Glimpse.* New York: HarperCollings, 1995, January 16 (non-numbered pages.)

32   The notion of bringing the mind home is found throughout the teachings of the historical Buddha as well as in many texts on the nature of meditation and the nature of mind. It refers to the process whereby one brings one's cognition, purely, to the awareness of mind itself without elaborations or fabrications. Easier said than done, perhaps, but worthy of consideration when working with the mind and meditation.

33   This quote came up in conversation with a friend when I was discuss-ing the nature of distractions and how to deal with them. I will find the source and post it on my web/blog as soon as I can.

34   There is a famous teaching by Sakyamuni Buddha entitled the *Pra-jnaparamita Sutra* (*prajna* (wisdom) *paramita* (perfection) in which the "ul-timate" way of being is elucidated through a series of verses that negate our normal way of looking at things. Hence, "beyond words, beyond thoughts, beyond description" is the mind when it is not caught in a fixed way of per-ceiving things and has gone beyond the conventional sense of mind. Again, while this may be abstract or incomprehensible to all but a few of us, knowing one's mind in a less distracted and more peaceful way moves one toward this way of being.

35   Dalai Lama. *Ethics for the New Millennium*. New York: Riverhead Books, 1999, pg. 124.

36   Please see footnote #18 for a discussion on the origination of this quote.

37   Rinpoche, Sogyal. *The Tibetan Book of Living and Dying*. San Fran-cisco: Harper Collins, 2002, pg. 187.

38   Rinpoche, Sogyal. *The Tibetan Book of Living and Dying*. San Fran-cisco: Harper Collins, 2002, pg. 203.

39   Kabat-Zinn, Jon. *Full Catastrophe Living—Using the Wisdom of Your Body and Mind to Face Stress, Pain, and Illness.* New York: Dell Publishing, 1990, pg. 345. This book is a must for anyone wanting to further their knowl-edge regarding the uses of mindfulness in the context of health care as well as their personal life.

40   Needleman, Jacob. *A Sense of the Cosmos: The Encounter of Modern Science and Ancient Truth.* Rhinebeck: Monkfish Book Publishing, 2003, p. 98.

41   Jung YH, Kang DH, Jang JH, Park HY, Byun MS, Kwon SJ, Jang GE, Lee US, An SC, Kwon JS. "The Effects of Mind-Body Training on Stress Re-duction, Positive Affect, and Plasma Catecholamines." Neuroscience Letters, 2010 Jul 26;479(2):138–42..

42   Needleman, Jacob. A Sense of the Cosmos: The Encounter of Modern Science and Ancient Truth. Rhinebeck: Monkfish Book Publishing, 2003, p. 98.

43   The Mind & Life Institute is a nonprofit organization that seeks to un-derstand the human mind and the benefits of contemplative practices through an integrated mode of knowing that combines first-person knowledge from the

world's contemplative traditions with methods and findings from contemporary scientific inquiry. Ultimately, their goal is to relieve human suffering and advance well-being.

44   Lutz A, Brefczynski-Lewis J, Johnstone T, Davidson RJ. "Regulation of the Neural Circuitry of Emotion by Compassion Meditation: Effects of Meditative Expertise." PLoS ONE, March 2008, Volume 3 Issue 3 e1897.

ABSTRACT:

Recent brain-imaging studies using functional magnetic resonance imaging (fMRI) have implicated insula and anterior cingulate cortices in the empathic response to another's pain. However, virtually nothing is known about the impact of the voluntary generation of compassion on this network. To investigate these questions we assessed brain activity using fMRI while novice and expert meditation practitioners generated a loving-kindness-compassion meditation state. To probe affective reactivity, we presented emotional and neutral sounds during the meditation and comparison periods. Our main hypothesis was that the concern for others cultivated during this form of meditation enhances affective processing, in particular in response to sounds of distress, and that this response to emotional sounds is modulated by the degree of meditation training. The presentation of the emotional sounds was associated with increased pupil diameter and activation of limbic regions (insula and cingulate cortices) during meditation (versus rest). During meditation, activation in insula was greater during presentation of negative sounds than positive or neutral sounds in expert than it was in novice meditators. The strength of activation in insula was also associated with self-reported intensity of the meditation for both groups. These results support the role of the limbic circuitry in emotion sharing. The comparison between meditation vs. rest states between experts and novices also showed increased activation in amygdala, right temporo-parietal junction (TPJ), and right posterior superior temporal sulcus (pSTS) in response to all sounds, suggesting greater detection of the emotional sounds and enhanced mentation in response to emotional human vocalizations for experts than novices during meditation. Together these data indicate that the mental expertise to cultivate positive emotion alters the activation of circuitries previously linked to empathy and theory of mind in response to emotional stimuli.

45   Lutz A, Greischar LL, Perlman D, Davidson RJ. "BOLD Signal in Insula Is Differentially Related to Cardiac Function During Compassion 2 Meditation in Experts vs. Novices. Neuroimage, 2009 Sep;47(3):1038–46.

ABSTRACT:

The brain and the cardiovascular system influence each other during the processing of emotion. The study of the interactions of these systems during emotion regulation has been limited in human functional neuroimaging, despite its potential importance for physical health. We have previously reported that mental expertise in cultivation of compassion alters the activation of circuits linked with empathy and theory of mind in response to emotional stimuli. Guided by the finding that heart rate increases more during blocks of compassion meditation than neutral states, especially for experts, we examined the interaction between state (compassion vs. neutral) and group (novice, expert) on the relation between heart rate and BOLD signal during presentation of emotional sounds presented during each state. Our findings revealed that BOLD signal in the right middle insula showed a significant association with heart rate (HR) across state and group. This association was stronger in the left middle/posterior insula when experts were compared to novices. The positive coupling of HR and BOLD was higher within the compassion state than within the neutral state in the dorsal anterior cingulate cortex for both groups, underlining the role of this region in the modulation of bodily arousal states. This state effect was stronger for experts than novices in somatosensory cortices and the right inferior parietal lobule (group by state interaction). These data confirm that compassion enhances the emotional and somatosensory brain representations of others' emotions and that this effect is modulated by expertise. Future studies are needed to further investigate the impact of compassion training on these circuits.

46   Slagter HA, Lutz A, Greischar LL, Francis AD, Nieuwenhuis S, Davis JM, Davidson RJ. "Mental Training Affects Distribution of Limited Brain Resources." PLos Biology, 2007 Jun;5(6):e138.

ABSTRACT:

The information-processing capacity of the human mind is limited, as is evidenced by the so-called "attentional-blink" deficit: when two targets (T1 and T2) embedded in a rapid stream of events are presented in close temporal proximity, the second target is often not seen. This deficit is believed to result from competition between the two targets for limited attentional resources. Here we show, using performance in an attentional-blink task and scalp-recorded brain potentials, that meditation, or mental training, affects the distribution of limited brain resources. Three months of intensive mental training resulted in a smaller attentional blink and reduced brain-resource allocation to the first target, as reflected by a smaller T1-elicited P3b, a brain-potential index of resource allocation. Furthermore, those individuals who showed the largest decrease in brain-resource allocation to T1 generally showed the greatest reduction in attentional-blink size. These observations provide novel support for the view that the ability to accurately identify T2 depends upon the efficient deployment of resources to T1. The results also demonstrate that mental training can result in increased control over the distribution of limited brain resources. Our study supports the idea that plasticity in brain and mental function exists throughout life and illustrates the usefulness of systematic mental training in the study of the human mind.

47   PNAS November 16, 2004 vol. 101 no. 46 16369–16373. This article is available online at the website for the Proceedings of the National Academy of Sciences - http://www.pnas.org/

48   Kabat-Zinn, Jon. Coming to Our Senses. New York: Hyperion, 2005, pg. 375.

49   Rosenzweig S, Greeson JM, Reibel DK, Green JS, Jasser SA, Beasley D. "Mindfulness-Based Stress Reduction for Chronic Pain Conditions: Variation in Treatment Outcomes and Role of Home Meditation Practice. Journal of Psychosomatic Research, 2010 Jan;68(1):29–36.

OBJECTIVE: This study compared changes in bodily pain, health-related quality of life (HRQoL), and psychological symptoms during an eight-week mindfulness-based stress-reduction (MBSR) program among groups of participants with different chronic-pain conditions.

METHODS: From 1997–2003, a longitudinal investigation of chronic-pain patients (n=133) was nested within a larger prospective cohort study of heterogeneous patients participating in MBSR at a university-based Integrative Medicine center. Measures included the Short-Form 36 Health Survey and Symptom Checklist-90-Revised. Paired T tests were used to compare pre/post changes on outcome measures. Differences in treatment-effect sizes were compared as a function of chronic-pain condition. Correlations were examined between outcome parameters and home meditation practice.

RESULTS: Outcomes differed in significance and magnitude across common chronic-pain conditions. Diagnostic subgroups of patients with arthritis, back/neck pain, or two or more comorbid pain conditions demonstrated a significant change in pain intensity and functional limitations due to pain following MBSR. Participants with arthritis showed the largest treatment effects for HRQoL and psychological distress. Patients with chronic headache/migraine experienced the smallest improvement in pain and HRQoL. Patients with fibromyalgia had the smallest improvement in psychological distress. Greater home meditation practice was associated with improvement on several outcome measures, including overall psychological distress, somatization symptoms, and self-rated health, but not pain and other quality of life scales.

CONCLUSION: MBSR treatment effects on pain, HRQoL, and psychological well-being vary as a function of chronic pain condition and compliance with home meditation practice.

50 Kimbrough E, Magyari T, Langenberg P, Chesney M, Berman B. "Mindfulness Intervention for Child Abuse Survivors." Journal of Clinical Psychology, 2010 Jan;66(1);17–33.

Twenty-seven adult survivors of childhood sexual abuse participated in a pilot study comprising an eight-week mindfulness meditation-based stress-reduction (MBSR) program and daily home practice of mindfulness skills. Three refresher classes were provided through final follow-up at 24 weeks. Assessments of depressive symptoms, post-traumatic stress disorder (PTSD), anxiety, and mindfulness were conducted at baseline, 4, 8, and 24 weeks. At eight weeks, depressive symptoms were reduced by 65%. Statistically significant improvements were observed in all outcomes post-MBSR, with effect sizes above 1.0. Improvements were largely sustained until 24 weeks. Of three PTSD symptom criteria, symptoms of avoidance/numbing were most greatly reduced. Compliance to class attendance and home practice was high, with the intervention proving safe and acceptable to participants. These results warrant further investigation of the MBSR approach in a randomized, controlled trial in this patient population.

51 Birnie K, Garland SN, Carlson LE. "Psychological Benefits for Cancer Patients and Their Partners Participating in Mindfulness-Based Stress Reduction (MBSR)." Psychooncology, 2010 Sep;19(9):1004-9.

OBJECTIVE: Cancer patients experience many negative psychological symptoms, including stress, anxiety, and depression. This distress is not limited to the patient, as their partners also experience many psychological challenges. Mindfulness-based stress-reduction (MBSR) programs have demonstrated clinical benefit for a variety of chronic illnesses, including cancer. This is the first study to report MBSR participation with partners of cancer patients.

METHODS: This study examined the impact of an eight-week MBSR program for 21 couples who attended the program together on outcomes of mood disturbance, symptoms of stress, and mindfulness. RESULTS: Significant reductions for both patients and partners in mood disturbance (p<0.05) and the Calgary Symptoms of Stress Inventory (C-SOSI) subscales of muscle tension (p<0.01), neurological/GI (p<0.05), and upper respiratory (p<0.01) symptoms were observed after program participation. Significant increases in mindfulness (p<0.05) were also reported in both groups. No significant correlations were observed between patient and partner scores on any measures at baseline or on change scores pre- to postintervention; however, after MBSR participation couples' scores on the Profile of Mood States and C-SOSI were more highly correlated with one another. Postintervention, partners' mood disturbance scores were significantly positively correlated with patients' symptoms of stress and negatively correlated with patients' levels of mindfulness.

CONCLUSIONS: Overall, the MBSR program was helpful for improving psychological functioning and mindfulness for both members of the couple. Several avenues of future research are suggested to further explore potential benefits of joint couple attendance in the MBSR program.

52   Biegel GM, Brown KW, Shapiro SL, Schubert CM. "Mindfulness-Based Stress Reduction for the Treatment of Adolescent Psychiatric Outpatients: A Randomized Clinical Trial." Journal of Consulting and Clinical Psychology, 2009 Oct;77(5):855–66.

Research has shown that mindfulness-based treatment interventions may be effective for a range of mental and physical health disorders in adult populations, but little is known about the effectiveness of such interventions for treating adolescent conditions. The present randomized clinical trial was designed to assess the effect of the mindfulness-based stress-reduction (MBSR) program for adolescents age 14 to 18 years with heterogeneous diagnoses in an outpatient psychiatric facility (intent-to-treat N = 102). Relative to treatment-as-usual control participants, those receiving MBSR self-reported reduced symptoms of anxiety, depression, and somatic distress and increased self-esteem and sleep quality. Of clinical significance, the MBSR group showed a higher percentage of diagnostic improvement over the five-month study period and significant increases in global assessment of functioning scores relative to controls, as rated by condition-naïve clinicians. These results were found in both completer and intent-to-treat samples. The findings provide evidence that MBSR may be a beneficial adjunct to outpatient mental-health treatment for adolescents.

53   Deyo M, Wilson KA, Ong J, Koopman C. "Mindfulness and Rumination: Does Mindfulness Training Lead to Reductions in the Ruminative Thinking Associated with Depression?" Explore (NY), 2009 Sep/Oct;5(5):265–71.

The purpose of this study was to investigate the impact of mindfulness-based stress-reduction training on a self-selected adult community sample in the areas of mindfulness, rumination, depressive symptomatology, and overall well-being. Targeting rumination was considered particularly important because a tendency toward rumination in nondepressed populations has been found to be predictive of subsequent onset of depression. As hypothesized, completers of the MBSR class showed increases in mindfulness and overall well-being and decreases in rumination and symptoms of depression. Limitations of the study are discussed, as are the implications of these findings.

54   Lush E, Salmon P, Floyd A, Studts JL, Weissbecker I, Sephton SE. "Mindfulness Meditation for Symptom Reduction in Fibromyalgia: Psychophysiological Correlates." Journal of Clinical Psychology in Medical Settings, 2009 Jun;16(2):200–7.

OBJECTIVES: Fibromyalgia, a chronic-pain syndrome, is often accompanied by psychological distress and increased basal sympathetic tone. In a previous report it was shown that mindfulness-based stress-reduction (MBSR) reduced depressive symptoms in patients with fibromyalgia with gains maintained at two months' follow-up (Sephton et al., Arthr Rheum 57:77–85, 2007). This second study explores the effects of MBSR on basal sympathetic (SNS) activation among women with fibromyalgia.

METHODS: Participants (n = 24) responded to a television news appearance, newspaper, and radio advertisements. Effects on anxiety, depressive symptoms, and SNS activation measures were tested before and after MBSR using a within-subjects design.

RESULTS: The MBSR treatment significantly reduced basal electrodermal (skin conductance level; SCL) activity (t = 3.298, p = .005) and SCL activity during meditation (t = 4.389, p =.001), consistent with reduced SNS activation.

CONCLUSIONS: In this small sample, basal SNS activity was reduced following MBSR treatment. Future studies should assess how MBSR may help reduce negative psychological symptoms and attenuate SNS activation in fibromyalgia. Further clarification of psychological and physiological responses associated with fibromyalgia may lead to more beneficial treatment.

55   Lengacher CA, Johnson-Mallard V, Post-White J, Moscoso MS, Jacobsen PB, Klein TW, Widen RH, Fitzgerald SG, Shelton MM, Barta M, Goodman M, Cox CE, Kip KE. "Randomized Controlled Trial of Mindfulness-Based Stress Reduction (MBSR) for Survivors of Breast Cancer." Psychooncology, 2009 Dec;18(12):1261–72.

OBJECTIVES: Considerable morbidity persists among survivors of breast cancer (BC), including high levels of psychological stress, anxiety, depression, fear of recurrence, and physical symptoms (including pain, fatigue, sleep disturbances, and impaired quality of life). Effective interventions are needed during this difficult transitional period.

METHODS: We conducted a randomized controlled trial of 84 female BC survivors (Stages 0–III) recruited from the H. Lee Moffitt Cancer and Research Institute. All subjects were within 18 months of treatment completion with surgery and adjuvant radiation and/or chemotherapy. Subjects were randomly assigned to a six-week MBSR program designed to self-regulate arousal to stressful circumstances or symptoms (n=41) or to usual care (n=43). Outcome measures compared at six weeks by random assignment included validated measures of psychological status (depression, anxiety, perceived stress, fear of recurrence, optimism, social support) and psychological and physical subscales of quality of life (SF-36).

RESULTS: Compared with usual care, subjects assigned to MBSR(BC) had significantly lower (two-sided p<0.05) adjusted mean levels of depression (6.3 vs. 9.6), anxiety (28.3 vs. 33.0), and fear of recurrence (9.3 vs. 11.6) at six weeks, along with higher energy (53.5 vs. 49.2), physical functioning (50.1 vs. 47.0), and physical role functioning (49.1 vs. 42.8). In stratified analyses, subjects more compliant with MBSR tended to experience greater improvements in measures of energy and physical functioning.

CONCLUSIONS: Among BC survivors within 18 months of treatment completion, a six-week MBSR(BC) program resulted in significant improvements in psychological status and quality of life compared with usual care.

56   Davidson RJ, Kabat-Zinn J, Schumacher MS, Rosenkranz BA, Muller D, Santorelli SF, Urbanowski F, Harrington A, Bonus K, Sheridan JF. "Alterations in Immune Function Produced by Mindfulness Meditation." Psychosomatic Medicine. 65:564–570. 2003.

57   The Center for Health Design (http://www.healthdesign.org/) is one such organization that has made great strides in providing education and advancement in the science and knowledge base of health-care design. Go to their website and check out the White Papers available for download. Alternatively, you can also find them on my website under the resources page.

58   Sternberg, Esther. *Healing Spaces*. Cambridge: The Belknap Press of Harvard University Press, 2009, pg. 293.

59   The asclepieion at Epidaurus was one of the most celebrated healing centers of the Classical world. Those will ailments and illnesses sought out this temple as a place where they could be cured and would spend the night in the enkoimitiria, a big sleeping hall, in hopes of finding a cure for their ailments. It was believed that during the night, in their dreams, the god himself would advise them what they had to do to regain their health. Found within of the

sanctuary at Epidaurus was a guest house with a capacity for up to 160 guests. There are also mineral springs in the vicinity that may have been used in healing.

60   Kabat-Zinn, Jon. *Coming to Our Senses*. New York, Hyperion, 2005. Pg. 358.

61   For a beautifully written journey into the realm of space and its healing qualities, Esther Sternberg's *Healing Spaces: The Science of Place and Well-Being* handles this subject in a fine and eloquent form.

62   Moustaka, E., Constantinidis, T. "Sources and Effects of Work-Related Stress in Nursing." *Health Science Journal*, V.4, Issue 4, 2010, pgs. 210–216.

INTRODUCTION: The working environment is one of the most important causes of occupational stress. The importance of management of occupational stress is recognized by occupational health and safety personnel since it has been found to be related not only with loss of productivity and loss of working hours but with the arousal of diseases and occupational accidents.

PURPOSE: The aim of this systematic review was the examination of the sources and consequences of occupational stress on nurses' adequacy, productivity, and efficiency.

METHOD: A systematic review was made in the websites for the "European Agency for Safety and Health at Work", the "National Institute for Occupational Safety and Health (NIOSH)", the "Job Stress Network" as well as the websites for the "Occupational and Environmental Medicine Journal" and various publications and abstracts using as key words «stress, occupational stress, and Nursing.

RESULTS: A number of aspects of working life have been linked to stress. Aspects of the work itself can be stressful, namely work overload and role-based factors, such as lack of power, role ambiguity, and role conflict. Threats to career development and achievement—including threat of redundancy, being undervalued, and unclear promotion prospects—are stressful. Stress is associated with reduced efficiency, decreased capacity to perform, and a lack of concern for the organization

CONCLUSIONS: During last decade there has been increasing recognition of the stress experienced by hospital nursing staff. Although some stressful situations are specific to a particular type of hospital unit, nurses are subject to more general stress that arises from the physical, psychological, and social aspects of the work environment. High levels of stress result in staff burnout and turnover and adversely affect patient care. Interventions that are targeted at sources of occupational stress seem to be required in order to support nurses.

63   J. K. Mojoyinola. "Effects of Job Stress on Health, Personal and Work Behaviour of Nurses in Public Hospitals in Ibadan Metropolis, Nigeria." *Ethno-Medicine*, 2(2): 143–148 (2008)

ABSTRACT:

The study investigated the effects of job stress on the physical health, mental health and personal and work behaviors of nurses in public hospitals in Ibadan Metropolis, Nigeria. It aimed at addressing the issue of how stress at work can be effectively managed, reduced, or prevented by the government and hospital management boards in order to enhance the health of the nurses as well as improve their personal and work behaviors. The study was carried out among 153 nurses working in two public hospitals in Ibadan Metropolis, Nigeria. Ex-post-facto research design was adopted for the study. A single questionnaire tagged "Stress Assessment Questionnaire for Hospital Nurses" (SAQFHN) was developed and used for the study. It contained 72 items, measuring demographic variables, job stress, physical and mental symptoms, and personal and work behavior. Two hypotheses were formulated and tested in the study, using analysis of variance and independent T-test. The study established that job stress has significant effect on physical and mental health of the nurses. It also established that there was a significant difference in personal and work behavior of highly stressed nurses and less stressed nurses. Based on these findings, it was recommended that the government (Federal or State) and Hospital Management Boards should improve the welfare of the nurses. It was also recommended that their morale should be boosted by involving them in policy or decision-making concerning their welfare or care of their patients. Their salary should be reviewed, and they should be promoted as when due.

64   Wicks, Robert. *Overcoming Secondary Stress in Medical and Nursing Practice*. New York: Oxford University Press, 2006, pg. 114.

65   Bae SH, Mark B, Fried B. "Use of Temporary Nurses and Nurse and Patient Safety Outcomes in Acute Care Hospital Units." *Health Care Management Review*, 2010 Oct–Dec;35(4):333–44.

BACKGROUND: To deal with nursing shortages and inadequate hospital nurse staffing, many solutions have been tried, including utilizing temporary nurses. Relatively little attention has been given to use of temporary nurses and its association with both nurse and patients outcomes.

PURPOSE: The purpose of this study is to investigate the association between the use of temporary nurses and nurse injuries (needlesticks and back injuries) and patient safety outcomes,(patient falls and medication errors) at the nursing unit level.

METHODOLOGY/APPROACH: Data came from a large organizational study that investigated the relationship between registered nurse (RN) staffing adequacy, work environments, organizational, and patient outcomes. The sample for this study was 4,954 RNs on 277 nursing units in 142 hospitals.

FINDINGS: Nurses working on nursing units with high levels (more than 15%) of external temporary RN hours were more likely to report back injuries than nurses working on nursing units that did not use external temporary RNs. Nurses working on these nursing units also reported greater levels of patient falls compared with those who did not use temporary RNs. This study found that nurses working on nursing units with moderate levels (5–15%) of external temporary RN hours reported fewer medication errors than those not using any external temporary RNs.

PRACTICE IMPLICATIONS: Hospitals need to monitor the levels of temporary nurse use and maintain a level of approximately 15% to ensure both nurse and patient safety outcomes. The use of temporary nurses to manage nursing shortfalls may provide both benefit and harm to nurse and patient safety depending on the level of the use.

66   Sternberg, Esther. *Healing Spaces*. Cambridge: The Belknap Press of Harvard University Press, 2009, pg. 295.

67   The Center for Health Design (http://www.healthdesign.org/) is one such organization that has made great strides in providing education and advancement in the science and knowledge base of health-care design. Go to their website and check out the White Papers available for download. Alternatively, you can also find them on my website under the resources page.

68   Rinpoche, Chokyi Nyima, Shlim, David R. *Medicine and Compassion—A Tibetan Lama's Guidance for Caregivers*. Boston: Wisdom Publications, 2004, pg. 145.

69   Longaker, Christine. *Facing Death and Finding Ho*pe. New York: Doubleday, 1997. pg. xv

70   Sternberg, Esther. *Healing Spaces*. Cambridge: The Belknap Press of Harvard University Press, 2009, pg. 295.

71   Groopman, Jerome. *The Measure of Our Days*. New York: Penguin Books, 1997, pg. 226.

72   Campbell, Joseph. *The Power of Myth*. New York: Doubleday, 1988, pg. 151.

73   The Greek use of the word *skandalon* in mythology often referred to the struggle or "hero's journey," to quote Campbell, that one encountered in

order to transcend or go beyond the regimented and normalized life. Within it was the potential for receiving a gift, either literal or psychological, and it was one's journey to find that gift.

74 Santorelli, Saki. *Heal Thy Self.* New York: Bell Tower, 1999, pg. 12.

Index

A

acceptance
  death, 137, 143
  experiences, 2
  habits, 85
  work environment as practice, 134
affirmation, 2–6
agape, 42
Ali, Asghar, 43
Asclepiades of Bithynia, 129
attachment, 24, 58, 60, 104, 140
attention. See meditative awareness
Austin, James, 30, 45–46, 69–70, 126
awareness. See also meditative
        awareness
  application in the workplace, 2–4,
        72–73
  exercises, 68–69, 73–74
  foundation for compassion, 67–68
  helps patients heal, 48–50
  imminence of, 70
  and meditation, 16–18
  and thoughts, 24

B

Barclay, William, 42
Beginning with Your Thoughts exercise,
        32–33
brain research, 119–128
"Brain-Wave Vibration" study, 119
breath
  mindfully attending to, 12–14
  one-breath meditation, 3–4
  riding, 14–16
Buddha, 41, 44
Buddhism, 62, 152, 154
burnout, 2, 4, 5

C

Caird, G.B., 42
Campbell, Joseph, 105, 149, 151
caring. See also compassion
  for the dying, 150
  genuine, 4
  motivation for, 1, 3
  for peers, 51
Caring for a Loved One exercise, 47–48
catecholamines, 119
Chokyi Nyima Rinpoche, 50, 137
Christianity, 42,105. See also Jesus
        Christ
chronic illness, 25–26
clouds as analogy for thoughts, 22–25
cognizance
  awareness, 59
  compassion, 29
  knowing quality, 62
  overseeing, 70
  unimpeded, 81
Collinge, William, x
compassion
  arousing, 47–48, 51–53
  and death, 137–146
  defined, 4

exercise, 105–109
and the healthcare profession, 46–47
reasons for lagging, 39–40
religious and spiritual traditions,
    41–46
seeing another as self, 46–47
compassionate presence
defined, 40
patients, positive effect on, 49–50
universality of, 28–29
creating stories, 58

D
Dalai Lama, 44, 99, 120–121
Davidson, Richard, 122–124, 124–125
death, 114, 115, 137–146
diagnoses, terminal, 25–26, 81–82,
    140–144
distractions. See also forgiving ourselves
exercise to return to mindfulness,
    15–17
and natural simplicity, 9
noticing, 29–30, 85–87
remaining free from, 11
thought-provoking exercise, 88–89
working with, 59, 87–88

E
The Effects of Mind-Body Training
    on Stress Reduction,
    Positive Affect, and Plasma
    Catecholamines, 119
Einstein, Albert, 45
emotions. See also compassion
dwelling on, 24–26
happiness, 100–109
identifying with, 23–24, 34
love, 41–42, 47–48
of patients, 22–23
working through, 95–97
empathy, 25–26
emptiness of self, 94
end of life. See death

enkoimitiria, 130
environment. See healing spaces
Epidaurus, 130–131

F
Finley, James, 39, 40, 41, 71, 155
focus. See mindfulness
forgiving ourselves, 17, 50–51, 92, 108,
    150
Fuller, Margaret, xxi

G
Goldstein, Joseph, 58, 70
Greek mythology, 105
Gregory of Nyssa, 153
grief after diagnosis, 25–26

H
happiness, 100–109
healing spaces, 129–136
health-care environment, 130–136
Hinduism, 44
hospitals, 129–136

I
immune response study, 124–125
impermanence, 27, 58–60, 80, 137
integration of meditation in life, 24, 41,
    57, 151,
interdependence with others, 50, 94, 101
Islam, 43

J
Jesus Christ, 41, 105, 121
Judaism, 42–43

K
Kabat-Zinn, Jon, 34, 104, 124–125, 131
Krishnamurti, J., 71–72

L
Lerner, Michael, 43
Longaker, Christine, 143
love
 for all people, 42
 evoking feelings of, 47–48, 51
 of self, 41
Loving-Kindness Practice exercise,
 51–53

M
Maidu, 130
medicine. See also diagnoses, terminal;
 immune response study
 aesthetics of health-care institutions,
 130–136
 lack of compassion, 46
 mind-body studies, 120–121, 126
meditation. See also mindfulness
 defined, 10–11
 one-breath, 3–4
 purpose of, 9
 research, 119–128
 three pillars, 67–69
meditative awareness
 defined, 10–11
 riding the breath, 12–17
 universality of, 28–29
memento mori, 137
Merton, Thomas, 55
metacognition. See cognizance
Milarepa, 142
mind as the forerunner of healing
 environment, 129–136
mindfulness
 application in the workplace, 2–4,
 72–73, 134
 and death, 137–146
 defined, 9–12
 discipline, 114
 exercises, 68–69, 73–74
 foundation for compassion, 67–68
 importance of, 69–70

practicing, 111–118, 147–157,
 159–164
universality of, 28–29
work as invitation to, 32
Mindfulness, Awareness, and
 Spaciousness in Meditation
 exercise, 68–69
Mindfulness Based Stress Reduction®
 (MBSR), 124–125
monks study, 123–124
motivation, 1–7
Muslim religion, 43–44

N
natural simplicity, 9, 10, 145
nature
 Buddha, 150, 154
 changing, 24, 91–92, 95
 compassionate, 5, 50, 68
 deeper, xii, 11, 73, 152
 divine, 150
 inherent, 50, 68, 101, 133, 150
 of mind, 88, 133, 150, 152, 154
 transient, 27, 80, 95, 97
 true, xix, 9, 73, 153
Needleman, Jacob, 111, 114, 120
nonattachment. See attachment
nurses and nursing. See also
 compassion; self; stress; who
 we are
 attending to the emotional well-being
 of patients, 94–95
 burnout, 2, 5
 caring for those we dislike, 109
 helping patients work with their
 minds, 82–83
 mindfulness, awareness and
 spaciousness use, 72, 144
 relationship with peers, 51
 stress in the work environment,
 132–135
 and suffering, 25–26, 100–109
 target of patients' emotions, 22

Riding the Breath exercise, 14–16
Rumi, Melvana Jelaludin, 77, 156

O
one-breath meditation, 3–4

P
Pascal, Blaise, 79–80
patients
 awareness helps heal, 48–50
 compassionate presence, positive
  effect of, 49–50
 emotions of, 22–23, 94–95
 helping them work with their minds,
  82–83
 mindfulness practice, 144
 and suffering, 100–109
 and terminal illness, 25–26, 81–82,
  140–144
 we dislike, 109
practicing mindfulness
 author's experience, 147–157
 how to, 159–160
 opportunities, 111–118, 163–164
 schedule, 161–162
Prajnaparamita, 152
Prometheus, 105
Psalm 90, 145
purity of perception, 29–30

Q
Qur'an, 43–44

R
Ramakrishna, 112–113
Ramon, Juan Jimenez, 91, 92
religious traditions, 28–29, 41–46,
  139, 149. See also Buddhism;
  Christianity
remaining, 60–61, 63–64
research, 119–128
respectful presence. See compassionate
  presence

S
Santorelli, Saki, 151
Schuman, Marjorie, 9
seeing
 another as another self, 47, 102
 beyond our limitations, 46
 leave the seeing in the seeing, 57
 suffering mirrored, 26
 transience of phenomena, 27
 with an undistracted mind, 22
self. See also who we are
 emptiness of, 94
 forgiving, 17, 50–51, 92, 108, 150
 genuine, 9, 68,
 impermanence of, 60
 inseparable nature with others, 50,
  60, 101–102, 151
 preoccupation with, 2, 9, 23
 seeing another as, 46–47, 100–102
self-love, 39, 41
self-mirroring mystery, 151
self-perception, 27–29
Shantideva, 44–45
Shlim, David, 46
skandalon, 149
Sogyal Rinpoche, xii, 4, 10, 18, 34, 85,
  154
spaciousness
 application in the workplace, 40,
  72–73
 breaking down barrier between self
  and other, 60
 and death, 137–146
 defined, 71–74
 exercises, 68–69, 73–74
 foundation for compassion, 67–68
 free from concerns, 9–11, 17
spiritual practices, 41–46, 139, 149
spiritually-based foundation, 41–42
state of simply being, 10–11

Sternberg, Esther, 130–131, 134–135, 144

stories in our mind, 29, 97

stress
  and acceptance, 21–25
  reaffirming motivation, 5
  and research into the mind, 119, 124
  and self-perception, 29
  in the work environment, 132

suffering
  of the caregiver, 25–26
  freedom from, 100–109

T

Tao, 152

teachers of meditation, 154–155, 171–179

terminal illness, 25–26, 81–82, 140–144

testing by God or nature, 149

thought-provoking exercise, 88–89

thoughts. See also distractions
  ability to be present, 57
  beginning exercise, 32–33
  being alone with, 77–84
  clouds as analogy for, 22–25
  creating stories, 58
  impermanence, 58–60
  increasing, 34–35
  releasing, 28
  remaining, 60–61, 63–64
  terminal diagnosis exercise, 81–82
  transformation of mind, 26–28, 56–57
  without a thinker, 62

The Tibetan Book of Living and Dying, 102–103

tonglen, 105–109

train station metaphor, 24–25, 58

Training in a Compassionate Impulse exercise, 78–79

transformation of mind, 26–28, 56–57

Tulku Urgyen Rinpoche, 88

V

vaccine study, 124–125

W

water if not stirred, 30

waves as analogy for thoughts, 63, 87-88

website, 14

when to practice, 14, 87–88, 111–118

who we are. See also self; thoughts
  changing nature of, 91–98
  defies description, 93
  dwelling on thoughts and emotions, 24–26
  emptiness of self, 94
  identifying with our thoughts and emotions, 23–24, 34
  interdependence with others, 94
  learning to be mindful, 30–35
  need to control external forces, 21–22
  patients' thoughts and emotions, 22–23
  purity of perception, 29–30
  transformation of mind, 26–28
  universality of mindfulness, 28–29

Wicks, Robert, 48–50, 132

Working with Difficult Thoughts and Emotions exercise, 95–96

Working with Dying exercise, 140–142

Working with Our Thoughts exercise, 60–61

workplace, 3, 82, 109, 131–134

Y

Yongey Mingyur Rinpoche, 24

Z

Zen and the Brain, 30, 45, 126